# Self-Esteem:
# A Classroom Affair

## 101 Ways to Help Children Like Themselves

# Michele and Craig Borba

1817

Harper & Row, Publishers, San Francisco

New York, Grand Rapids, Philadelphia, St. Louis
London, Singapore, Sydney, Tokyo, Toronto

Cover illustration by
Constance Crawford.

Illustrated by Constance Crawford;
additional artwork by Chris Larson.

Library of Congress Catalog
    Card Number: 78-50396
ISBN: 0-86683-612-8
(previously ISBN: 0-03-043906-X)
        90  9

# Acknowledgments

Acknowledgments of quotes are given
in the order they appear on the chapter
title pages.

Daniel Ungaro, *How to Create a
Better Understanding of Our Schools*
(Minneapolis, Minn.: T. S. Denison,
1959), p. 20.  Used by permission.

Muriel James and Dorothy Jongeward,
*Born to Win: Transactional Analysis
with Gestalt Experiments* (Reading,
Mass.:  Addison-Wesley, 1971), p. 1.
Used by permission of the publisher.

David Elkind, *Children and Adolescents:
Interpretive Essays on Jean Piaget,*
2nd ed. (New York: Oxford University
Press, 1974), p. 57.  Used by permission.

Rachel L. Carson, *The Sense of
Wonder* (New York: Harper & Row,
1956), p. 42. Copyright 1956 by Rachel
L. Carson. Reprinted by permission of
Marie Rodell-Frances Collin Literary
Agency.

William Glasser, *Schools Without
Failure* (New York: Harper & Row,
1969), p. 13.  Used by permission.

Robert C. Hawley and Isabel L. Hawley,
*Human Values in the Classroom:
Teaching for Personal and Social Growth*
(New York: Hart, 1975),  p. 89.  Used
by permission.

William W. Purkey, Sr.,  *Self-Concept
and School Achievement*  (Englewood
Cliffs, N.J.: Prentice-Hall,  1970), p. 26.
Used by permission.

With special love to Mom and Dad—the real self-image experts!

Special thanks to Peggy Dwyer, Cindy Morse, Nancy Shipcott, and Mary Grace Galvin for their support and encouragement and to my little friends at Congress Springs School who taught me what real specialness is.

# Table of Contents

# Foreword

It's all here. A book for teachers of young children, and we've been waiting for it. The Borbas have woven together a brilliant tapestry of exercises and strategies that will make even the most fatigued teacher a charismatic wonder.

Based on sound, eclectic theory, the activities have practical applications that will make thousands of children happy the Borbas were born. There isn't an idea in here that hasn't been tested on children. The book exudes a special sense that everything is tried and true.

Probably the nicest thing I can say is that I wish my teacher had had this book in his or her magic file when I was a kindergarten kid. How self-enhanced I would have become.

Sidney B. Simon
Professor of Humanistic Education
University of Massachusetts
January 12, 1978

# Preface

Creating an environment in which children learn to like themselves is, in our opinion, a major, contemporary educational challenge. We are strongly convinced that both behavioral and academic growth are the direct results of environments in which children have the opportunity to internalize positive self-images. In fact, we feel a positive, self-enhancing atmosphere is essential to a child's educational success.

In *Self-Esteem: A Classroom Affair,* we share activities and ideas that have helped us create such an atmosphere. Each activity is complete within itself but also adapts to use with most academic subjects. Since communication skills are so essential to successful interaction and the maintenance of self-esteem, the activities in this book are designed to help children gain confidence in their ability to communicate both verbally and in written form.

The activities in *Self-Esteem: A Classroom Affair* were field-tested for five years in a public classroom and in a private clinical setting. The children in both settings had enjoyable experiences and felt successful. As a result, we are convinced others can easily incorporate these activities and ideas into their work with children. Not only classroom and special-education teachers but also early childhood-education personnel, counselors, resource specialists, program developers, and parents will find the materials helpful. We welcome the opportunity to conduct inservice training sessions and to present our ideas and activities to teachers and leaders interested in affective child development.

We are constantly reminded that each child is a precious human being with great potential. To develop this potential, children need to challenge their abilities and their limits, to hear praise for their accomplishments, and to feel accepted by the people with whom they daily work and learn. As teachers we want to be part of this challenge, praise, and acceptance so each child with whom we work will develop a more positive self-concept. We hope these activities make it easier and more fun for you to join us in helping children learn to like themselves.

Happy Helping!

Michele and Craig Borba
655 West Middle Avenue
Morgan Hill, CA 95037

# Chapter One
# Introduction

Pupils differ greatly in interests, abilities, and cultural backgrounds. Pupils mature physically, mentally, emotionally, and socially at different rates of speed. They vary in rates of learning and in their attitudes toward learning. Success in their work is necessary for their own self-esteem . . . They should have confidence in their ability to grow. A child must feel that he is understood and appreciated for what he is as well as for what he accomplishes . . . When children are happy they radiate this happiness everywhere they go.

Daniel Ungaro
*How to Create a Better Understanding of Our Schools*

# What Is Self-Concept?

Self-concept is the consolidation of all the information received from a person's environment—a person's perceptions of how he or she is viewed by others and how he or she sees him or herself. Consequently, environmental and social experiences play a significant role in the building and molding of a child's self-concept. For example, a child interprets positive reactions to his or her person as I am good and negative reactions as I am not good. Subsequently, he or she integrates the accompanying feelings of worth or worthlessness into his or her self-image. Therefore, when a child says, "That's me!" he or she is referring to the many attitudes, beliefs, values, ideas, and perceptions that make up his or her total self-concept.

# Why Is Affective Education Important?

At one time or another all of us hear children say, "I'm no good." Negative experiences lead some children to conclude that they are and will remain of little worth. As a result, these children see no point in trying to learn new concepts and skills. Despite our efforts to emphasize their positive qualities and to help them develop their full potential, their negative self-image limits their success.

Although studies reveal that positive attitudes can effect change in a child's negative self-image, the older a child is the more difficult it becomes for him or her to change. Early childhood education is, therefore, a crucial stage and an optimal time for affective learning. For example, the earlier a child learns that failure is not bad in itself but is rather a natural part of the learning and living process, the easier it will become for the child to cope with failure and develop feelings of adequacy that maximize his or her educational success. Or when the message that you are a worthwhile individual permeates and underscores each interaction between teacher and student, feelings of self-worth will develop and eventually be reflected in student attitudes.

Psychological research concerning self-esteem shows strong correlation between a child's self-image and his or her academic success. The research of child psychologist Stanley Coopersmith shows that self-esteem is a better predictor than intelligence test scores of a child's future academic success. Psychologist William Morse concurs, having found that self-esteem was the better predictor of lower elementary students' reading readiness.

Since self-esteem so strongly influences cognitive growth, we believe that attention to affective learning should be an integral rather than supplementary part of the standard curriculum. An integrated affective/cognitive curriculum creates a well-balanced educational environment that helps children develop their full human potential.

In *The Authentic Teacher,* Clark Moustakas capsulizes our conviction. "By cherishing and holding the child in absolute esteem, the teacher is establishing an environment that facilitates growth and becoming."[1]

1. Clark Moustakas, *The Authentic Teacher: Sensitivity and Awareness in the Classroom* (Cambridge, Mass.: Howard A. Doyle, 1966), p. 13.

# The Importance of Significant Others

The first day of kindergarten is a milestone in the lives of children—a day when they begin to forge ahead toward independence in a new environment. Parents and family will no longer be the only primary persons in the child's life. Others—those teachers, friends, and peers whom a child considers significant—begin to influence and affect development of the child's self-concept. If these new significant others consider and treat the child as a worthwhile and an important human being, they will help the child develop a positive self-image.

# School-Enhancing Activities

Include the entire staff and school in self-image building activities in order to help children develop positive attitudes toward the world outside their classroom.

At the beginning of each school year, take extended walks within the school building. Invariably, touring upper-grade rooms starts children thinking about the future.

Select a staff-member-for-the-week and have the children interview that person about his or her job. Be sure to include people in nonteaching and nonadministrative roles; for example, janitors, nurses, secretaries, bus drivers, cafeteria workers. Remember staff members whom you honor with thank-you notes, pictures, or other mementos.

Invite the principal to visit frequently in your classroom, to chat with the children, to do a special lesson, or to read a book to the children.

Invite older children to assist you by providing cross-age tutoring.

Have special achievers visit another classroom to share their accomplishments.

Invite another class to visit your classroom. During the visit, point out special projects that have stimulated positive actions in your classroom.

# Things to Remember!

A positive attitude is contagious! If the children hear you say positive things about their peers, they too will begin to think and comment positively. So start each day on a positive note and remember that even a seemingly insignificant achievement is worth a positive comment.

Consistency is essential. Children feel more secure when they know what is expected of them. Stick to the rules you set for your students.

One goal of affective education is to help children increase their self-confidence by making it possible for them to reveal their weaknesses and fears as well as their strengths and talents—without fear of rejection. Therefore, avoid making value judgments by being accepting of the children's responses.

Nonparticipation in group discussions is okay. A child, like an adult, may not always feel secure enough to participate. Perhaps next time, he or she will feel more confident.

Positive attitudes and behavior don't develop overnight. They result from consistent effort on everyone's part. Be assured, however, that your efforts are worthwhile and that change will occur. Patience will win the day.

Remember, they're children! So help them enjoy life as they discover the beauty in themselves, in others, and in the world around them.

# Hints for Using This Book

Since the activities in *Self-Esteem: A Classroom Affair* can be used with children of many ages in a wide range of situations, the teacher who constantly seeks ways to adapt the material and suggestions in the book will reap the greatest benefit from it.

**Writing (printing) and reading.** You may need or prefer to write (print) and read for some children, especially beginning elementary children and the learning handicapped. However, be sure to let the children do the creating. They can dictate their thoughts to you (or to a classroom helper). Keep this in mind even when the specific activity directions do not indicate the option.

**Activity center.** The activities in *Self-Esteem* require the use of materials and equipment that the children will not have at their desks, and many activities will require a large working surface. Therefore, we recommend that you set up an activity center in which the children can find these supplies and where they can work on their projects.

**Concept circles.** We often ask the children in our classes to gather together in a circle when we give directions, introduce a project, discuss a topic, or share reactions and responses. We call these talking and sharing times "concept circles," or we specify the purpose by calling them sharing or discovery circles.

Sitting in a circle helps the children concentrate on the discussion and creates a feeling of unity and support among the children as well as between the children and their teacher or leader. Consider using this seating arrangement even when a *Self-Esteem* activity doesn't specifically suggest it.

**Reproducible pages.** Many activities in *Self-Esteem* are meant to be reproduced and distributed to the children. Permission is given by the publisher to reproduce these pages for classroom use. In most cases a short explanation precedes the chart, puppet outline, letter, or award. Cut off or cover this material when you duplicate the page for the children's use.

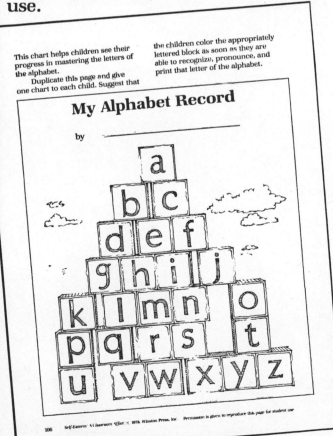

This chart helps children see their progress in mastering the letters of the alphabet.
Duplicate this page and give one chart to each child. Suggest that the children color the appropriately lettered block as soon as they are able to recognize, pronounce, and print that letter of the alphabet.

**My Alphabet Record**

by _____

a
b c
d e f
g h i j
k l m n o
p q r s t
u v w x y z

106   Self-Esteem: A Classroom Affair © 1978. Winston Press, Inc.   Permission is given to reproduce this page for student use

**Role playing.** Several *Self-Esteem* activities suggest that you ask the children to role play. Role playing is different from both acting out stories and creative dramatics since it requires children to think of and to act out a solution to a problem situation. Children can role play dilemmas, classroom conflicts, or story situations. Role playing is a valuable technique for allowing children to put themselves in the place of another and for helping them learn to make decisions. Consider the following suggestions for effective role playing:

• Wait until class members are acquainted with one another and at ease with you before introducing role playing.

• Choose a dilemma or story situation that's relevant to the children's lives and that has a number of realistic but not obvious solutions.

• Announce that the purpose of the role play is to find a solution to the problem.

• Emphasize that the children must deal with the situation as it is stated rather than change the situation to create a solution.

• Avoid role-playing situations that might invade a child's privacy. However, if misunderstanding occurs or feelings get hurt, be warm, sensitive, and responsive.

• Invite children to volunteer for the role play, but only after they have thought of a possible solution.

- Caution children not to hurt one another physically, especially when role-playing situations become highly active.

- Involve children who are observing the role play by urging them to listen carefully and to ask themselves, Could that really happen? What would I do? Is there another way to solve the problem?

- Anticipate some self-consciousness (evidenced perhaps by giggling and silliness) when role playing is first introduced. Tell the children that you felt awkward too the first time you did a role play. Then remind them that the purpose of the activity is to see if their solutions really work and that role playing gives them a chance to test out their ideas.

- Stop the role playing when the children find a solution. Also stop the role playing when personal conflict arises. Be sure to ask those involved to share their feelings. When an impasse occurs, discontinue the role play and ask if anyone else has an idea he or she wants to try out.

- Discuss the role-played solution with all the children. Invite them to think about the solution's possible consequences. Ask, Is the solution a good one? Why? Why not?

- Encourage the children to think of (or to role play) other alternatives.

- Conclude the role-playing session by helping the children evaluate their solutions. Ask, Which is the best solution? Which is the worst? Why?

If a role-playing session is not successful, ask yourself, Did I acquaint the children well with the technique of role playing? Did I describe the dilemma or story situation clearly? Did the children have enough time to think of possible solutions before I asked them to volunteer for the role play? Then apply what you learn from an unsuccessful attempt to improve the next role-playing session.

# Chapter Two

# An Enhancing Environment

Each human being is born as something new, something that never existed before. He is born with what he needs to win at life. Each person in his own way can see, hear, touch, taste, and think for himself. Each has his own unique potentials—his capabilities and limitations. Each can be a significant, thinking, aware, and creatively productive person in his own right—a winner.

Muriel James and Dorothy Jongeward
*Born to Win: Transactional Analysis with Gestalt Experiments*

# Create an Enhancing Environment

The activities presented in this chapter suggest ways to make the classroom an environment that allows for, stimulates, and fosters the growth of positive self-image.

## Teach Children to Praise Themselves

A child's feelings of adequacy and self-acceptance are central to the success of the whole educational process. When children feel good about themselves, their motivation is higher and they become more involved in everything they do. As a result, they retain and make use of what they learn over a longer period of time.

Since significant others provide the data from which a child derives much of his or her self-perception, teachers can do a great deal in the classroom to help children internalize a positive self-image. If teachers do this, the children will also be successful in their learning.

However, in order to catch positive attitudes, children need models to imitate. Be a positive model by praising yourself in front of the children. If children often hear you make statements, such as "I did a good job on this lesson today," they'll begin to internalize the positive value judgment. No fair cheating though! Children also need to learn that their models make mistakes. If you've done a poor job, admit it by saying, for example, "I surely didn't organize myself well today!"

Often, children with negative self-images really don't know how to speak positively. You'll need to help them see and feel their successes. Whenever success occurs, help the child verbalize the success. Soon, making positive statements will become more automatic. With continued support and reinforcement, the child will internalize a positive attitude.

## Beat Those Dark and Dreary Days

To ease the tension caused by the grumpiness and depression that children as well as adults occasionally feel, establish the following very simple classroom procedure. For every negative thing a child says, ask him or her to say one positive thing. After a successful experience with this technique, ask for the children's cooperation and make it a classroom rule. Consistently remind the children when they forget the rule.

When you are in a grumpy mood, let the children know by writing your name and *Beware, I've got the grumpies!* on the chalkboard. Encourage the children to do the same.

Remember that smiles and happiness are infectious, so for those exceptionally dark days, use a jolly classroom mascot, such as a smiling clown or a favorite animal puppet

*Eric, I think you really did a nice job on this paper. Tell yourself that.*

*I really did a nice job on this paper.*

to remind children to smile and that their smiles can make other people happy, too.

Select a child who is particularly happy and smiling and put the mascot by him or her. Ask the child to pass the mascot on when he or she finds another happy classmate.

## Structure Classroom Procedure to Enhance Self-Image

In *Antecedents of Self-Esteem,* Stanley Coopersmith states that children brought up in an environment structured by definite, controlled limits tend to develop more self-esteem than those reared in a more permissive atmosphere. Coopersmith concludes that "well-defined limits provide the child with a basis for evaluating his present performance as well as facilitating comparisons with prior behavior and attitudes."[1]

Most children, and particularly the learning disabled, need and want the structure of defined goals. Since definite, stated goals eliminate uncertainty and make meeting expectations easier, school and life become more enjoyable. The following paragraphs present ideas for structuring classroom procedure to enhance children's self-image.

1. Stanley Coopersmith, *Antecedents of Self-Esteem* (San Francisco: W. H. Freeman, 1967), p. 237.

- At the beginning of each day, ask the children to gather in a circle. Explain clearly what you expect of them for the day. Remember to ask if they have any questions about your expectations.

- Let the children know in advance what the consequences will be if they don't meet your expectations. Don't pull any surprises!

- To help the children remember activity objectives, provide visual aids; for example, picture or word charts that remind children of the objectives by indicating the sequence of steps in an assigned activity.

- At the end of each instruction period, form an evaluation circle. Encourage the children to share what they just learned and to discuss any problems or questions that arose during the instruction. Conclude the evaluation by restating your expectations for the remainder of the day.

- Be available each day for conferences with the children. Have children who want to talk privately with you sign their names in a designated place on the chalkboard or in an appointment book.

- Provide the children with contracts that indicate what each child is expected to complete within an allotted time.

- Provide an area where children can always go for a few quiet moments. Furnish the R & R (rest and relaxation) area with pillows, comfortable chairs, books, and stuffed animals. Children feel better about themselves when they see that other people also occasionally have difficulty controlling their emotions and need to spend time alone to get themselves back together. Remember your role as the children's behavior model and endorse the children's use of the R & R area by using it yourself.

# Begin and End with Friendliness

## Get-Acquainted Reception

Since beginning school is sometimes a scary experience (even the second and third time around), ease the uncertainty by immediately establishing a friendly environment with a get-acquainted reception.

Obtain the principal's permission to have a reception on the day before school begins. Then send a letter of introduction to the children, inviting them to attend a get-acquainted reception in their new classroom. Remember to give the date and the specific time. (Hold the reception to an hour or less.)

Keep the reception simple. Push two desks together and cover them with a paper tablecloth or with butcher paper. Arrange a centerpiece of fresh-cut flowers and provide treats and a beverage.

Warmly greet each child as he or she arrives. Solicit parent help with making name tags. (Have small pieces of paper, felt-tip pens, and safety pins available for this purpose.)

After everyone has had a snack, call the children together, make introductions, and tell them a story. Before the children leave, thank them for coming and express your anticipation of happy times to come.

# Welcome Letter

Lay the groundwork early for feelings of specialness that can contribute to building a positive self-image. Before the school year begins, mail a letter to each child who will be in your classroom. The letter will create in the child the expectation of a personalized and friendly classroom atmosphere. Having set up the expectation, be sure to follow through and pay specific attention to each child on the first day of school.

Dear _____,

   Hello!   My name is _____. I am going to be your new teacher. I'm really looking forward to the beginning of school and to meeting you. During the summer, I've been busy making lots of fun games and activities for our classroom.

   We're going to learn so many exciting things this year! We're going to learn how to read and how to do math. I'm especially excited because we're going to learn about why you're so special. Did you know that you're a very, very important person?

   I hope that you're having a fun summer. I can't wait to hear about what you've been doing, so before school begins, you'll receive an invitation to visit our classroom. I hope you'll come.

   See you in the fall.

            Fondly,

# End-of-the-Year Letter

End the year on a note of friendliness, too. Send the children a letter that reminds them of some of the activities you've done together and that comments on the children's growth and learning.

Dear _____,

    I want to tell you how much I enjoyed having you in my class this year. You worked hard to make our class time fun, and I feel we've become close friends.

    I expect it was a little scary the day you came to school and we met eachother for the first time. I remember how hard it was for you at first to use scissors, to color inside the lines, to write your letters, to learn your sounds, to hop and skip, and to jump rope. You've grown in so many ways since last fall. You should be very proud of yourself.

    I think it's exciting to look back and remember some of the special things we did. Do you remember
—when we made houses from milk cartons?
—when you learned to read and do math problems?
—our cooking projects, especially our Thanksgiving feast?
—our Mexican fiesta, the tacos, and the piñata?
—learning about dinosaurs?
—giving your first report?
—dyeing Easter eggs?
—our Indian play and making Pueblo Indian bread?
—our trip to the fire station?
—planting our indoor garden?
—our swimming party?

    It's nice to have you as a friend and it was nice to help you learn. I know you'll have a wonderful time next school year, too. I'll miss you very much.

                    Fondly,

 *Self-Esteem: A Classroom Affair,* © 1978, Winston Press, Inc.

# Plan Positive Actions Toward Others

## Mail a Letter to a Classmate

A child feels important when he or she receives a letter with his or her own name on the envelope. Create this excitement for your students by having them write letters to each other.

First, fill a hat with slips of paper on which the children have printed their names. Caution the children to keep the names they will draw a secret. Then, have each child draw one slip out of the hat. Next, have the children write a letter to the classmate, address the stamped envelope they brought from home, put the letter in the envelope, seal it, and place the envelope in the classroom letter box. (Remember to provide the children with a list of their classmates' home addresses.)

Locate a mailbox close to the school. When all the letters are written and ready to mail, walk with the children to the mailbox so they can personally mail the letters. If this is not possible, assure the children that you will mail the letters for them.

## Tape Friendly Messages

This activity is designed to boost children's self-esteem by sharing with them the taped compliments of classmates.

Set up a tape recorder in the activity center. Whenever a child wants to say a few friendly words about a classmate, encourage him or her to go to the center and record the message. (See "Reading Progress Tapes," page 105, for suggestions on using the tape recorder with elementary children.) During a concept circle, have the class listen to these surprise messages.

## Celebrate Birthdays

Special attention increases children's feelings of worth. Because birthdays are already extra-special days, they are a ready-made way to honor a student and affirm his or her sense of self-worth. Take care, however, to remember the birthday of every child in the class. Consider the following ways to celebrate the children's birthdays:

- Declare one hat a special birthday hat, which a child may take off the shelf and wear only on his or her birthday.

- Tape an "Our Birthday Friend" sign to the birthday child's chair.

- Stipulate that on birthdays children may bring treats to share with their classmates and teacher (one treat per person).

- Have classmates make a group card for the birthday friend. Fold a piece of construction paper in half. On the cover, print an inscription, such as *Friends Make It Seem Like Birthdays All Year Around*. On the inside of the card write Happy Birthday, _____. Invite the children to decorate the cover and to sign the card.

- Have a celebration for the children whose birthdays occur in the summer, too. Make a birthday crown for each of these children and have the remainder of the class provide the treats.

# Use Cross-Age Helpers

Cross-age helpers are typically two to three grade levels ahead of the children whom they tutor. These helpers provide you with extra classroom assistance and help build the self-esteem of the children with whom they work.

We find that children profit a great deal from cross-age tutoring and that the rapport which develops between the two children—the younger child and the tutor—during each session is a delight to observe. Invariably the younger child looks up to his or her older friend with awe and respect. You'll find your students counting the minutes until their teacher friends return for another session.

The task of cross-age helpers is to reinforce skills that you have already presented. Teach the helpers game techniques to use during their tutoring sessions. The helpers will often create stimulating and motivating games of their own. Encourage them to devise activities that reinforce skills. However, have the helpers check out their ideas with you before using them in the tutoring sessions.

Arrange regular talks with the tutors. Remember to praise them, answer any questions they have, discuss any problems they are having, and give them constructive suggestions for future sessions. We find that comments on the fantastic job the helpers are doing usually dominate these talk sessions.

# Make a Friendly Tree

*The Friendly Tree* activity organizes and encourages children to perform acts of friendliness that make the recipients feel good about themselves.

## Materials Needed
- construction paper
- a container, such as a two-pound coffee can
- tree branch
- spray paint
- sand or plaster of paris
- felt-tip markers
- paper punch
- yarn or cord
- scissors

The first step in making the Friendly Tree is to cover a container with colored construction paper on which you printed *The Friendly Tree.*

Find a tree branch large enough to hold several cards tied to its twigs. Spray the branch. Fill the container with sand or plaster of paris and place the tree branch in the container. If you use plaster of paris, provide support for the branch until the plaster dries.

Cut rectangular cards from colorful construction paper. On each card, print a friendly action, such as picking up scrap paper, smiling at a classmate, sharing a book, helping a classmate carry something. Punch a hole in the top of each card and tie the cards onto the tree with yarn or cord.

At the beginning of each day, invite each child to select a card on the tree and to read the friendly action printed on the card. (The children should leave the cards on the tree.) Then, ask the children to choose a person for whom they will do the friendly action. Encourage the children to select a different person each day.

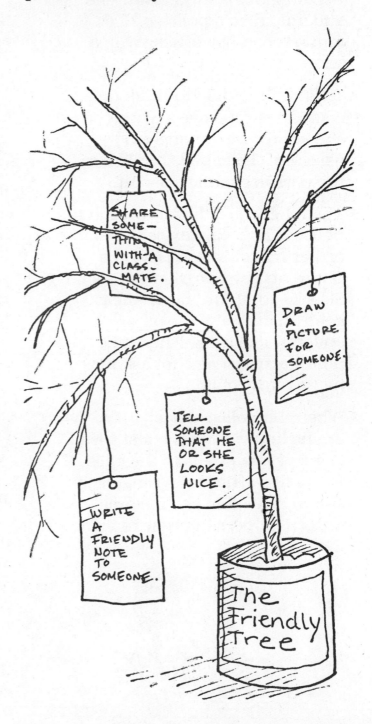

# Play "Police Officer, Have You Seen My Friend?"

Point out children's strengths by playing the game "Police Officer." Use the following rules:

• Ask for two volunteers, one to be a person looking for a lost friend and one to be a police officer. Equip the police officer with a badge.

• Tell the first child to think of someone in the class whom he or she knows well enough to describe. (The child should keep the person's name a secret.)

• Then, have the child approach the police officer and explain that his or her friend is lost. Have the police officer ask what the friend likes to do, things he or she is good at, and why the other children like him or her. (The police officer does not ask the name of the child.)

• When the police officer thinks he or she knows who the lost friend is, he or she points to the child. If the police officer is wrong, he or she may need to call in some official helpers in order to solve the case.

# Keep a Record to Help Remember

Activities and events that develop self-awareness and build self-esteem are well worth remembering. The five projects that follow suggest ways to remember.

## Class Journal

Remember meaningful things that happen in your classroom during the year by maintaining a record of visitors, field trips, and special happenings in a class journal. Keep the journal and pen or pencil on a classroom writing table and encourage the children to write comments at the time the events occur.

## Activity Time Line

To help your students recall successful activities you've done together during the year, create an activity time line.

Save samples of the children's project work throughout the year. Put up a wire or a clothesline cord; pin the project samples onto the wire in the order the children completed them.

# Photo Board or Scrapbook

To remember classroom events and each child's earlier appearance, make a photo board or photo scrapbook. Take photos of the children at various times throughout the year and keep a photo record of all your field trips and projects. Parents are apt to quickly contribute to the collection once they discover you have such a board or scrapbook.

If you choose to make a photo scrapbook, extend the activity by having the children dictate or write statements about each picture. If you write these comments on separate sheets of paper, cut out the comments and tape them next to the appropriate pictures.

Keep scrapbooks from previous years on display. You'll be surprised how many former students will return to look at the photos (and comments) in their old scrapbook.

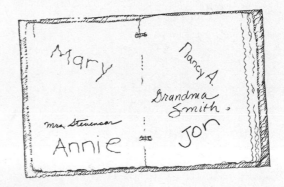

# Autographs

Suggest that the children make autograph books to help them remember friendships formed during the school year.

**Materials Needed**
- construction paper
- writing paper
- stapler
- paper punch
- yarn or cord

Have each child make an autograph book. First, have the children cut out a colorful construction paper cover in the shape of a favorite classroom object. Then have them cut out interior pages of matching size and shape. (Each booklet will need as many pages as there are children in the class.)

The children can staple the pages and cover together. Or they can bind the book by first punching two holes on one side of the booklet and then tying the pages and cover together with yarn or cord.

Invite the children to decorate the covers of their booklets.

Set aside time for the children to collect their friends' autographs, phone numbers, and addresses.

# A Book About My Friends

Suggest that each child in the class remember his or her classmates and teacher by making a construction paper scrapbook. The scrapbook should contain one page for each person in the classroom. (See "Autographs," page 17, for directions on how to make a scrapbook.)

At the top of each page in their scrapbooks, have the children print a classmate's name. Then tell them to fill the page with discoveries they have made about that person throughout the year; for example, what color that person's eyes are, things that person enjoys doing, games he or she likes to play, his or her favorite word, things he or she is good at, and his or her phone number and address.

# Chapter Three

# All-About-Me Activities

In large measure, most of our anxiety about the large number of unhappy and unsuccessful students in our schools is derived from a contemporary over-emphasis on intellectual growth to the exclusion of the personal-social side of development. Although I know it sounds old-fashioned to talk about the "whole child" and "tender loving care," I strongly believe that most problems in child rearing and education could be avoided if the adult's concern for a child's achievement as a student were balanced by an equally strong concern for his feelings of self-worth as a person.

Dr. David Elkind
*Children and Adolescents*

# Learning About Self

Self-esteem increases in an environment that provides opportunities for growth and success. As a significant other for the children in your room, you greatly affect whether such opportunities are present. However, since the children themselves are often significant others for each other, they also greatly influence the self-esteem building quality of their classroom environment.

Since children must value themselves before they can relate positively to one another and can value each other in a way that promotes self-esteem, these activities are designed to help the children first recognize their own uniqueness, especially physical characteristics that make them special and one-of-a-kind. Simultaneously, the activities assist the children to recognize the uniqueness of their classmates.

# Developing Physical Awareness

## Growth Chart and Picture Time Line

Charting the physical growth of elementary children draws attention to their appearance and helps them see how their bodies are developing. When children feel good about their bodies, they also tend to feel good about themselves psychologically and socially.

However, children often equate physical growth with personal worth. Help them to understand that self-worth is not dependent on physical size.

**Making a growth chart.** Record your students' growth in height on a chart posted in an easily visible classroom place. Print the title *Wow! Am I Growing!* at the top of the chart. During the first week of school, write the name and mark the height of each child on the chart. Remeasure and mark the children's height at regular intervals throughout the school year.

**Making a picture time line.** Another way for children to observe and record their growth is on a picture time line. Write the title *Wow! Have I Changed!* at the top of an unlined 12″ x 18″ piece of paper (along the 18″ side). Then, divide the paper into four vertical sections and label them *Me as a Baby, Me a Year Ago, Me Now,* and *Me Later.* Duplicate this paper; make one for each child in the classroom

Have the children draw pictures or illustrate each section with snapshots of themselves. Also encourage them to write or dictate incidents experienced or hoped for during each of these time spans.

Depending on the sophistication of your class, increase or decrease the number of time segments on the picture time line.

## "Me" Prints

In order to emphasize children's uniqueness, have each child convert a self-portrait into a fingerpaint print.

**Materials Needed**
- white construction paper
- popsicle sticks
- fingerpaints
- craft smocks (optional)

Ask the children to use bright colors (orange and green are very effective) to cover the entire surface of a large sheet of white construction paper with a free-form fingerpainting. While the fingerpainting is still wet, have each child use a popsicle stick to scratch out a picture of his or her face.

Give each child a second sheet of construction paper. Have them gently place this second sheet over the fingerpainting, match the sides, and lightly rub over the entire sheet of paper. When the children separate the sheets of paper, they will see prints of themselves on the second sheets.

After the prints are dry, ask each child to look at him or herself in the mirror and compare that image with the one on the print.

## Mirror Drawings

Children require a great deal of time to become aware of the various parts of their bodies and of how these parts are proportioned. Since children can rarely resist looking at themselves in a mirror, having a full-length mirror in your room will help them develop physical self-awareness. Encourage mirror usage by having the children make mirror drawings.

### Materials Needed
- full-length wall or free-standing mirror
- masking tape or white shoe polish
- 12" x 18" construction paper
- pencils
- color crayons or felt-tip markers

Put a strip of masking tape on the floor a few feet in front of the mirror. Divide the mirror into four

equal parts and mark the division with a strip of masking tape or a line of white shoe polish. Have the children stand behind the strip of masking tape on the floor, look at themselves in the mirror, and observe which parts of their bodies they see in each of the four sections.

Give each child a 12" x 18" piece of construction paper folded lengthwise into four equal parts. With pencils, have the children draw what they see in each mirror section on the corresponding section of the folded construction paper. When the children are satisfied that their proportions are correct, have them trace the sketches with felt-tip markers or color crayons.

# "Me" Paper Dolls

Self-awareness is an integral component of self-concept. Young children can develop physical self-awareness by making and displaying doll replicas of themselves. The dolls will help them notice, think about, and increase appreciation for their own physical characteristics.

Help the children observe objectively. If they exaggerate or caricature certain traits, elicit their feelings about those traits. Acknowledge negative feelings about awkward traits or physical handicaps but encourage the children to concentrate on changing what is changeable.

## Materials Needed
- tagboard paper-doll pattern
- butcher paper
- scissors
- buttons, rickrack, yarn, cord
- fabric or wallpaper remnants
- acrylic paint and brushes, felt-tip markers, or color crayons
- newspapers
- stapler
- paper punch (optional)

Provide the children with a large tagboard paper-doll pattern. Have each child trace two paper dolls onto butcher paper — a front and a back — and cut out the dolls.

From the bric-a-brac you provide, have the children create dolls that look like themselves. They'll make clothes, paint skin tones and facial features, and draw the shoes. Remind the children to dress the backs of the dolls, too.

When the dolls are completed, help the children staple the front and back together, limb by limb, stuffing each part of the doll's body with small, crumpled pieces of newspaper.

If you plan to display the dolls by hanging them up, punch a hole at the top of each doll's head. For easy hanging, give the children a loop of colorful yarn or cord that they can thread through the hole.

# "Me" Cloth Dolls

Making these dolls draws attention to children's physical traits and provides an opportunity for encouraging children to take pride in their appearance and to be self-accepting about their bodies.

## Materials Needed
- 8½" x 10½" white drawing paper
- fabric crayons
- iron
- skin-colored fabric
- large-eye needles
- #10 sewing thread
- cotton batting or cotton balls
- sewing machine (optional)

With fabric crayons (available in stationery or wallpaper stores) have the children draw a free-hand picture of themselves on an 8½" x 10½" piece of paper. Tell the children that since they will stuff the dolls later, they should make the arms, legs, and neck wide enough to push the stuffing through.

Iron each child's picture onto one-half of an 11" x 18" piece of fabric that you have folded to a 9" x 11" size. Cut out the shape, being careful to allow at least one quarter of an inch extra material around the doll for seams.

With the right sides facing each other, join the two pieces of fabric on a sewing machine. Leave a 2" opening on one side of the body. Turn the pieces right-side out, have the children stuff the doll with cotton batting or cotton balls, and then whipstitch the 2" opening together. Or with the wrong sides facing each other, simply whipstitch the two pieces of fabric together, leaving a 2" opening for stuffing the doll. Remember to whipstitch the opening together after the children have stuffed the doll.

# Pictures of Differences and Similarities

This activity draws attention to the fact that children are not only unique and separate individuals but that they are also similar to other people.

Divide the class into pairs. Instruct each pair to think of eight ways the partners are alike and eight ways they are different.

Then ask the pairs to draw two pictures—one illustrating their similarities and one depicting their differences—and to write or dictate statements about the similarities and differences.

*We both have freckles and long hair.*

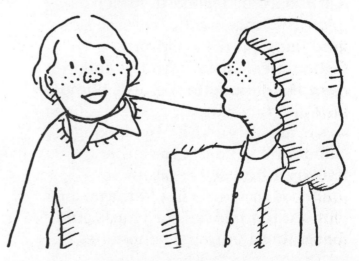

# Silhouette Pictures

One-of-a-kind items are highly sought after. Capitalize on this value judgment by making silhouette pictures to draw attention to children's individuality.

**Materials Needed**
- overhead projector
- black and white construction paper
- pencils
- scissors
- glue or paste
- 8½" x 11" cardboard or tagboard
- picture hangers
- old magazines (optional)

As each child stands in front of an overhead projector, trace the silhouette that appears on the wall onto a piece of black construction paper. (Consider using room helpers for this activity.)

Have the children cut out their own silhouettes, paste the black silhouette to a piece of white construction paper, and then mount the silhouette on a piece of cardboard or tagboard. Attach a picture hanger to the reverse side and hang up the children's silhouettes. Later, have the children take the silhouette pictures home or give them as gifts.

Vary this activity by making silhouette collages. Have the children find self-descriptive pictures or words in old magazines, cut out the pictures or words, and paste them onto the silhouettes.

Silhouette pictures also make good book covers. Consider them for the What-I-Can-Do books described on pages 32-33.

# Wanted Posters

Another way to develop self-awareness is for each child to make a personal wanted poster like the one illustrated.[1]

**Materials Needed**
- 12" x 18" construction paper
- camera (optional)
- drawing paper or typing paper
- pencils
- paste or glue

1. This activity was developed by Beverly Takeda.

Using the wanted poster on this page as a guide, make a poster for each child on a 12″ x 18″ piece of construction paper. Have each child fill in the identifying information about him or herself.

Take pictures of the children and attach them to the posters.

Or have the children choose partners, sketch each other's face, and paste these sketches to the posters.

At a parent night, cover the child's name and picture and ask each parent to identify his or her child's poster.

# Wanted!

Name __Brent Gale__

Height __4'3"__

Weight __56 lbs.__

Hair __Brown__

Eyes __Brown__

Likes to __Play soccer__

Can often be found __Outside__

Special talents __Making things__

# Fingerprints

The easiest and surest proof that no two people on this whole earth are alike is their fingerprints! Confirm children's uniqueness by having them take their own fingerprints.

**Materials Needed**
- fingerprint cards
- ink pads
- paper towels
- magnifying glasses (optional)

Show the children how to fingerprint themselves by pressing your finger onto an ink pad and then onto a sheet of scratch paper.

Duplicate the official classroom fingerprint card on this page and have each child fill out his or her own card, just as he or she would at the police station! Provide paper towels so the children can wipe off the ink that remains on their fingers.

Provide magnifying glasses and encourage the children to examine their fingerprints more closely. Have the children compare their fingerprints and note differences and similarities.

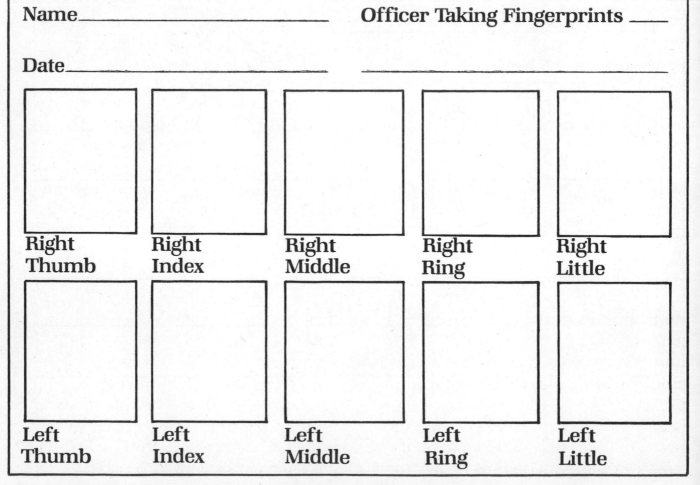

# Official Classroom Fingerprint Card

Name_____      Officer Taking Fingerprints ____

Date_____      _____

Right Thumb | Right Index | Right Middle | Right Ring | Right Little

Left Thumb | Left Index | Left Middle | Left Ring | Left Little

# Our Community Mural

To help the children learn about their own characteristics and to help them realize that there are many kinds of people and houses in their community, have each child make a paper replica of him or herself and of his or her house, which will become part of a class mural entitled *Our Community*.

## Materials Needed

- construction paper (include several house colors)
- mirror
- paper-doll pattern(s)
- cardboard (optional)
- wallpaper or fabric remnants
- various colored yarn scraps
- color crayons, felt-tip markers, acrylic paints and paint brushes, or fingerpaints
- scissors
- glue or paste
- stapler
- milk cartons (optional)

**Making the paper people.** Ask the children to examine themselves in the classroom mirror and to notice and comment on the shape and color of their physical features.

Provide paper-doll patterns of more than one size and shape in order to emphasize people's uniqueness. (If you want the children to create these patterns themselves, provide cardboard heavy enough to withstand use as a pattern. Give each child a piece of cardboard and invite him or her to draw a pattern that looks like his or her body.)

Have each child choose a paper-doll pattern that he or she thinks looks like him or herself. Show the children how to trace a pattern onto paper. Then, give them construction paper and tell them to trace around their paper-doll patterns. Have the children cut out the dolls.

Provide wallpaper or fabric remnants for making the doll clothes. Tell the children to cut out doll clothes that will fit their dolls and to paste or glue the clothes onto the dolls. Give them scraps of yarn to use for the hair.

Next, have the children paint or color in facial features that resemble their own. Encourage them to include freckles, scars, and other identifying marks.

**Making the houses.** The day before you begin this project, ask the children to go home and carefully look at the front of their houses. Ask them to notice where windows and doors are placed, what the color of the house and roof is, and where the chimney is located. The next day, ask each child to select an appropriately colored piece of construction paper and to draw the front of his or her house. Have the children cut out their houses.

Next, using the appropriate color paper, have each child draw and cut out a roof piece to fit the house. Show the children how to paste or glue a roof into place.

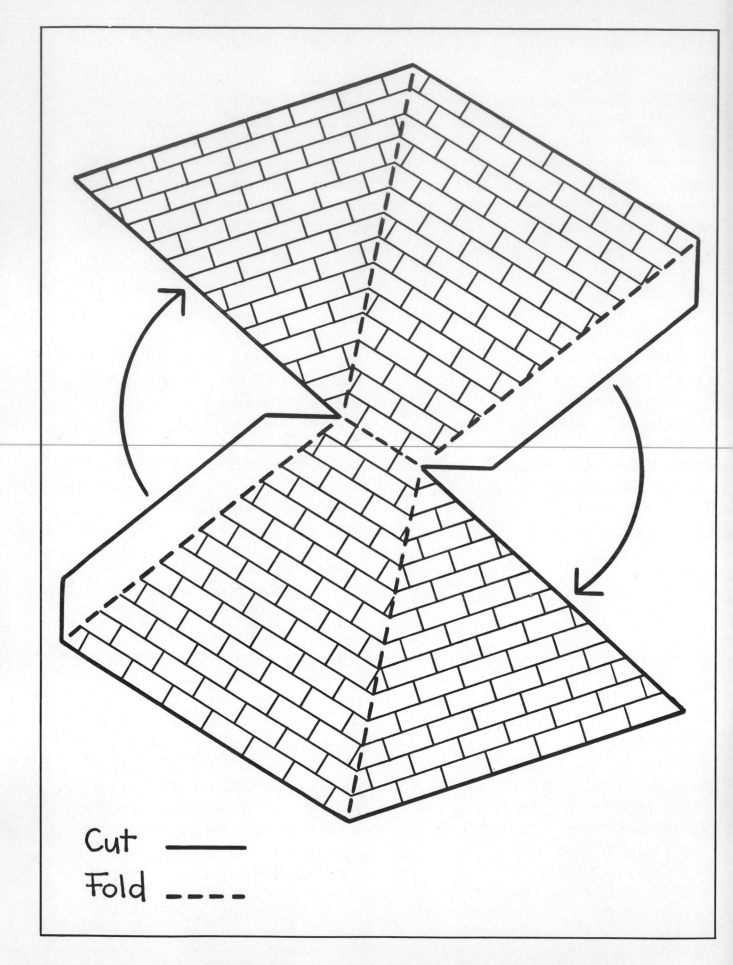

Cut _____

Fold _ _ _ _

Encourage the children to cut out paper windows and doors and to paste them on their houses. Remind them to provide their houses with chimneys.

For a three-dimensional mural, give each child the bottom part of a quart milk carton with which to construct a house replica. Ask each child to cover this milk carton with the color construction paper that is closest to the color of his or her house. From colored construction paper, have the children cut out roofs for their milk-carton houses. Staple the roof paper to the top of the halved milk carton. Then, have the children paste paper windows, doors, and chimneys to their milk-carton houses.

**Putting the mural together.** Have the children use butcher paper (or other sturdy paper available in large sheets) and prepare the background of the mural by painting or coloring the sky, hills, grass, and streets. Next, have them paste or glue the houses and the paper dolls into place. Finally, invite the children to draw trees and flowers on construction paper, to cut them out, and to paste them to the mural.

# Discovering Recipes

## People Recipes

Recipes differ just as children do. And many ingredients make up a recipe just as many personal characteristics make a child unique and special. Writing about personal traits in the style of a recipe can help children recognize and enjoy their uniqueness.

Use this activity following a cooking lesson in which the children learned about recipe terms, such as *teaspoons, cups, tablespoons, mix,* and *dash.*

Ask the children, What are you made of? Have them give their answers as a recipe. Then, ask the children to print and illustrate their recipes on 8½" x 11" sheets of paper. Compile the recipes in a *Book of People Recipes.* Also consider using individual recipes as parent gifts.

Recipe for Nancy
2 tbsp. niceness
1 tsp. naughtiness
dash of smiles
a few hugs
Mix the niceness and naughtiness. Add a dash of smiles and a few hugs. Bake well in the love and care of friends and of family.

## Ancestors' Recipes

A child's self-esteem grows roots when he or she develops ancestral pride. Learning about family backgrounds helps a child connect with his or her past and also develop appreciation and respect for the national and ethnic backgrounds of classmates.

Notify parents that their child will interview them about the family heritage and ask the parents to respond carefully to their child's questions.

In a concept circle about sharing, give the children an opportunity to tell what they learned about their ancestors. Provide a large world map, small pieces of paper, felt-tip markers, and push pins. After the children have printed their names on the pieces of paper, have each child pin his or her name tag to the country from which his or her family ancestors originated. Some children may need to print their names on several pieces of paper and pin these name tags to several countries.

To conclude your study, ask the children to bring ethnic foods to school for an ethnic luncheon. Encourage parents to let children help with the food preparation.

Extend this activity by collecting recipes for the foods brought to the luncheon and compiling them in a cookbook of ancestors' recipes. If possible, make a copy of the cookbook for each child.

# Expressing Feelings

## A Picture Dictionary of Feelings

Children need to learn the words that identify feelings, moods, and emotions. Collecting pictures for a book about feelings will help the children identify their own feelings and give them the vocabulary to verbalize their feelings.

**Materials Needed**
- two pieces of 12″ x 18″ tagboard
- several pieces of 12″ x 18″ paper
- old magazines
- paste or glue
- scissors
- color crayons

Make a 12″ x 18″ book entitled *A Picture Dictionary of Feelings*. Decorate a 12″ x 18″ piece of tagboard for the cover. At the top of each page in the book, write words that describe feelings and moods, such as *happy, sad, afraid, silly, mad, love, serious*.

Place the book in the activity center and have the children illustrate each emotion with pictures. Provide old magazines as source material but also encourage the children to draw original illustrations.

# Movement That Expresses Feelings

Music helps children identify moods. Being able to name feelings and moods helps children deal constructively with their feelings.

## Materials Needed
- recordings
- scarves
- mirror
- drawing paper
- water-color paints and brushes
- color crayons (optional)

Each day play a different musical selection. Have the children interpret the mood of the music by rhythmically moving their bodies to the music.

Vary the interpretive technique. Suggest dancing, finger dancing, mirror dancing (one child leads and the partner imitates the movements), or scarf dancing (the child moves a scarf to the rhythm and mood of the music).

Follow these interpretive sessions with a concept circle in which the children talk about the feelings they experienced while listening and moving to the music.

After the children have shared their experiences, suggest that they illustrate the mood of the music in a painting (or a color-crayon drawing).

Consider the following musical selections for eliciting the following feelings:

- I'm sad.
  Anton Dvořak, "Symphony No. 5 in E Minor"
  Peter Ilich Tchaikovsky, "Symphony No. 6 in B Minor (Pathétique)"

- I'm angry.
  Modest Mussorgsky, "Night on Bare Mountain"
  Edvard Grieg, "March of the Mountain King"
  Paul A. Dukas, "The Sorcerer's Apprentice"
  Claude Debussy, "The Sea (La Mer)"

- I'm happy.
  Peter Ilich Tchaikovsky, "Nutcracker Suite"
  Anton Dvořak, "Carnival Overture"
  Maurice Ravel, "Boléro"

- I'm playful.
  Camille Saint-Saëns, "Carnival of the Animals"

- I'm scared.
  Gustav Holst, "Mercury" from *The Planets*
  Edvard Grieg, "Peer Gynt"

- I'm happy and angry.
  Sergei Prokofiev, "Peter and the Wolf"

# Emphasizing Children's Strengths

Everyone likes to hear and feel that he or she is good at something. However, children with negative self-images do not often hear positive statements about themselves. Children with low self-esteem may not even realize they have characteristics to be proud of. Or they may actually not have developed any strengths to feel good about.

Since strengths develop first in areas of interest, collect information about your students' interests. Keep a paper and pencil handy to note interests you hear students talk about in concept circles or free conversation. During home conferences, take mental note of things students proudly show you.

Point out and emphasize children's strengths so they will be aware of their positive attributes. Say, for example, Johnny, did you know you're a super tap dancer?

## What-I-Can-Do Books

Having children make books that emphasize what they can already do will strengthen each child's sense of accomplishment and self-worth.

**Materials Needed**
- colorful construction paper
- writing paper
- scissors
- pencils
- paper punch
- yarn or cord
- glue or paste

Begin by having the children cut out two large circles from colorful construction paper for the covers and several identically-sized circles from writing paper for the inside pages.

Print the title *What I Can Do* on each cover and suggest that the children decorate their covers with cut-out flowers.

Tell the children to write on each page of their books a sentence stating one thing they do well. Have them begin each sentence with "I can. . . ." After the children have completed their books, punch holes on one side and tie the books together with yarn or cord.

Display the books on a bulletin board under the caption *I Can!*

**Writing other books.** Extend this activity by having your students write other books. They are experts on many topics, such as favorite toys, favorite school activities, favorite books, their wishes for the present and the future, their feelings.

# Favorite Activities Mobile

This mobile encourages pride in personal taste by drawing attention to the children's favorite activities.

## Materials Needed
● geometric tagboard patterns
● drawing paper
● crayons or acrylic paints and brushes
● old magazines
● glue or paste
● wire clothes hangers
● paper punch
● yarn or cord

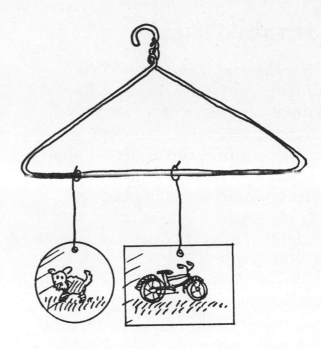

First, have the children trace around geometric tagboard patterns. Then invite them to draw pictures or to find examples in magazines of activities they enjoy. Have the children cut out these pictures and paste or glue them onto the front and the back of the geometric shapes.

Have each child bring a wire clothes hanger from home. To create the mobile, punch a hole at the top of each of the child's geometric shapes and tie these shapes onto the hanger with yarn or cord.

# A Hobby Display

In *The Clinical Treatment of the Problem Child,* Carl Rogers says, "With almost any child, the observant and understanding teacher can find some gift or talent or interest which the child may develop within the school room with some profit and much satisfaction . . . and thus a chance to win some approval."[2]

Provide this chance for approval by inviting the children to bring their hobbies to school and to display them for their classmates to see.

Also arrange an opportunity for each child to teach the other children about his or her hobby. The child can tell why he or she chose the hobby and where to obtain materials and reference books. Remember to leave time for questions and answers.

Invite another class to view the display and to learn, too.

2. Carl Rogers, *The Clinical Treatment of the Problem Child* (Boston, Mass.: Houghton Mifflin, 1939), p. 233.

# Chapter Four
# All-About-Me-and-My-Feelings Books

A child's life is like a piece of paper on which every passerby leaves a mark.

Ancient Chinese proverb

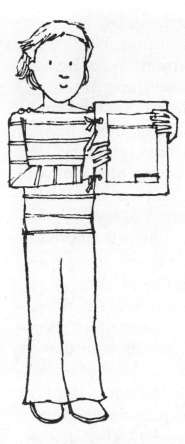

# Reproducible Book Pages

Use the remaining pages in this chapter to help the children in your classroom make delightful books about themselves. These pages will give them an opportunity to write about their feelings, their thoughts, their special likes, and their hopes. When the children complete their books, they will know themselves a little bit better and they will likely be proud of their authorship and value books more.

Since the topics about which the children will write deal primarily with feelings, we suggest you use this project after you've conducted several concept circles and other activities dealing with feelings. (See "Concept Circles," pages 51-72, and the activities on pages 30, 31, 110, and 111.)

Before you begin this project, duplicate pages 38-50. Make one copy of each page for every child in your classroom. Keep each child's duplicated pages and cover in a manila folder.

Begin the project by enthusiastically announcing that the children are going to make books about themselves. Show the children the folders and explain their uses. Tell the children that they will need several days to complete their books and that you will give them one page at a time to do. Express interest in reading the children's books when the books are finished.

Show the children several library books. Point out the titles, the authors' and illustrators' names, the publishers' names, and the copyright years.

For each child's book, duplicate on construction paper the cover illustrated on page 37. Give a book cover to each child and ask him or her to print on the cover the name of the author of the book (him or herself), the publisher (the school), and the copyright year.

To illustrate the cover, have each child draw a 4" x 6" picture of him or herself. Or take a picture of each child and suggest that the children paste these pictures in the cover box that is labeled *The Author*.

Now have the children fill in the interior pages of their books. Introduce no more than one topic

per day. On the day that the children write about a specific emotion or feeling, discuss it with them and show them pictures that illustrate the emotion or feeling. You can also read the children stories that portray the emotion being talked about. (Bibliotherapy for Children, pages 133-134.) Or role play some incidents that involve the feelings under discussion.

After the discussion, give the children the page that correlates with the emotion you discussed and invite them to write or dictate their completion of the topic statement; for example, on the page about anger, ask the children to complete the statement "I get mad when. . . ."

Sometime before the project is concluded, complete for each child's book the statement "I like having you in my class because. . . ."

At some point during the project, distribute the blank pages from the children's project folders. Tell the children that this page is one that will increase the uniqueness of their individual books because it will appear only in that one book. On this page, invite each child to write about something that he or she wants especially to include in his or her book.

# All About Me and My Feelings

## The Author

Author _____

Publisher _____

Copyright _____

I like having you in my class because

# I am a good friend when

# I get mad when

# I'm glad to be me because

# I am great because

# I like _____

# I am happy when

*Self-Esteem: A Classroom Affair,* © 1978, Winston Press, Inc.    Permission is given to reproduce this page for student use.

# In my school I like to

# When I grow up

*Self-Esteem: A Classroom Affair,* © 1978, Winston Press, Inc.   Permission is given to reproduce this page for student use.

# I feel silly when

# I feel sad when

*Self-Esteem: A Classroom Affair,* © 1978, Winston Press, Inc.    Permission is given to reproduce this page for student use.

# I get scared when

*Self-Esteem: A Classroom Affair,* © 1978, Winston Press, Inc.    Permission is given to reproduce this page for student use.

# Chapter Five
# Concept Circles

If you treat an individual as he is, he will stay as he is, but if you treat him as if he were what he ought to be and could be, he will become what he ought to be and could be.

Johann Wolfgang von Goethe

# What Are Concept Circles?

One of the techniques that we've found very successful in our teaching is the concept circle. We use the term *concept circle* to mean the time when the children gather in a circle and concentrate their thoughts and activity on one specific, designated idea or concept.

Concept circle time always seems to bring big, happy smiles to the faces of our students.

To insure good circle times, establish and explain the following ground rules to the children:

**Rule 1.** *Remain seated in the place you choose.* Have the children sit in a large circle on the floor. Sprinkle a little pretend glue on the floor to remind them not to move from their spots.

**Rule 2.** *Make only nice, friendly, true comments.* We call such comments "fuzzies."

**Rule 3.** *Talk only when it's your turn.* Use a pass-around prop to remind the group whose turn it is to speak.

**Rule 4.** *Plan your comment or answer during the thinking time.* To move circle activities along, set aside a few minutes early in the session as thinking time.

**Rule 5.** *Put your hands on your heads while instructions are given.* This posture helps children concentrate and remember your instructions.

# Self-Awareness Circles

The following three circle activities develop self-awareness and feelings of self-worth by requiring children to describe themselves positively.

## I'm Glad to Be Me

Use puppets as props for an *I'm Glad to Be Me* circle. (See page 74 for instructions on making *"Me" Puppets.*)

Begin the circle by having the first child say, "I'm glad to be me because. . . ." The next child then looks at his or her neighbor and says, "_____, you are glad to be you because. . . , and I'm glad to be me because. . . ." (Repeating their neighbor's statement helps the children think of themselves in relation to other people.) Repeat the process until all the children have participated.

## Mirror, Mirror

Use a hand mirror as the object to pass in this circle. Have each child look into the mirror and repeat the following verse:

> Mirror, mirror in my hand,
> Tell me why I'm the best child
>     in the land

After the child gives one reason why he or she is the best child in the land, have him or her pass the mirror to the person on his or her right.

## I'm Great

Give a few raisins to each child and have the children take turns popping the raisins into their mouths and mimicking Leo the Lion. Each child roars (but gently), "I'm GR-r-r-eat because. . . ," and completes the statement.

*I'm GR-r-r-eat!*

# Awareness-of-Others Circles

Extend self-awareness to awareness of others by using the next four circle activities to have children identify characteristics of their peers.

## People Riddles

On a 3″ x 5″ card, have each child draw a self-portrait, sign his or her name, and place the card on a bulletin board or in a pocket chart.

During the *People Riddles* circle, invite each child to make up a riddle to go with his or her self-portrait. For example:

I am a boy. I live in a blue house.
I like to play with blocks.
I color well. I like soccer.
Who am I?

Fold the riddles and put them into a hat. Then have each child draw a riddle out of the hat and have a volunteer begin the circle activity by reading the riddle he or she drew. Ask the other children to guess which classmate the riddle is about. Have the child indicate his or her guess by pointing to the appropriate self-portrait. When the guess is correct, tell him or her to pin the riddle to the board under the matching self-portrait card or to slip it into the appropriate pocket on the pocket chart. Then, ask the child who guessed correctly to read the next riddle.

Keep the self-portraits and their matching riddles on display for the remainder of the week.

# Classmate Flowers

To begin this activity, provide the children with precut flower centers and flower petals. Have each child decorate and print his or her name on a flower center. Display the flower centers so the children can later easily attach the flower petals to them.

During a series of concept circles, ask each child to share one discovery about a specific classmate, such as what he or she likes or doesn't like, what he or she does well, friendly things he or she does.

Have the children print their discoveries on the precut flower petals and attach the petals to the appropriate flower centers.

When the flowers are complete, suggest that the children take them home and proudly show them to friends and relatives.

PASTE TO FLOWER CENTER

*Self-Esteem: A Classroom Affair,* © 1978, Winston Press, Inc. Permission is given to reproduce this page for student use.

# Our Discovery Book

Make a book entitled *Our Discovery Book* which contains a page for every member of your class and one for yourself. Boldly print each child's name on a separate page in the book. Print the name in the top right-hand corner of the page. Colorfully decorate the book cover.

Introduce the word *discovery* when you first present the book to your class. Tell the children that a discovery is something you learn that you never knew before. Frequently use variations of the term *discovery* in the next few days. Point out discoveries you make about the children. Say, for example, "Tracy, I've made a discovery about you. I didn't know before that you liked to play checkers." The children will soon begin to make and share their own discoveries about others. Encourage and guide them into including discoveries about themselves, too.

Once the children are actively discovering, you are ready to gather information for the class discovery book. Gather in a *Discovery Book* circle and have each child dictate something he or she has discovered about him or herself. In a subsequent *Discovery Book* circle, have each child dictate one thing he or she has discovered about each classmate. Print these discoveries on the appropriate child's page in the discovery book. Remember to share your own self-discoveries and to include the children's discoveries about you on your page in the book.

When the discovery book is complete, announce a final *Discovery Book* circle and have the children read aloud from the book. Display the book in an accessible place and encourage the children to continue reading it and adding discoveries they make about themselves and their classmates.

# Talking Glasses

For this circle, pass an old pair of sunglasses. Have a child put the glasses on. His or her right-hand neighbor then says,

> Glasses, glasses, say what
>     you see;
> Tell what you like best
>     about me.

The wearer of the glasses answers for the glasses, says one nice thing about the person who recited the verse, removes the glasses, and passes them to his or her left-hand neighbor. Continue the process until all circle members have participated.

# Friendship Circles

The sense of self-worth that leads to self-esteem and positive self-concept doesn't develop in a vacuum, nor is it self-maintaining. Recurrent acknowledgment and confirmation of a person's worth is necessary in order to maintain the good feelings he or she has developed about him or herself. One of the easiest ways to affirm the worth of other people is to be friendly toward them.

## The Way to Be Friendly

In this activity the children discuss what it means to be friendly and decide which of a series of statements describe friendly actions.

Discuss with the children what the word *friendly* means. Print the sentences below on separate cards to be placed in the middle of the circle.

- Your friend pushes you down at recess.
- A classmate helps you with your work.
- Someone takes the ball away from you.
- A person smiles at you.
- Someone tells you that you look nice.
- A classmate tells you he doesn't like you.
- A friend sits with you at lunch.
- A classmate invites you over to her house to play.
- A friend tells you he doesn't want to play with you.
- Someone makes you a get-well card.
- A friend forgets your birthday.
- A classmate breaks your favorite toy.
- A friend helps you pick up the crayons.
- A friend shares her best toy with you.
- Someone pushes you out of the line.
- A classmate won't let you play in the game.
- A classmate calls you on the phone.
- Someone shares his snack with you.
- A friend tells you she likes your work.
- Someone calls you a bad name.
- A classmate helps you clean up.

Divide the class into teams of two and ask the partners to sit next to each other in the circle. Have each team pick a card, read it aloud, and decide if the statement describes a way to be friendly. If the team decides the statement depicts an unfriendly action, ask them to tell why they think the action is unfriendly and to correct the sentence so it describes a friendly action.

# Secret Buddies

Print the children's names on small pieces of paper, fold the papers, and place them in a hat.

Begin the *Secret Buddies* circle in the morning. Tell the children that they are going to draw names that they must keep secret. Pass the hat around and have each child draw the name of a classmate for whom he or she will be a secret buddy for the day. Explain that secret buddies make an extra effort to be friendly and helpful to the person whose name they've drawn.

Toward the end of the day, reassemble in the *Secret Buddies* circle. Have the children take turns describing friendly things that were done for them throughout the day. Ask each child how this made him or her feel and if he or she can guess who the secret buddy is.

# Fuzzy Comments

Gather the children in a circle. Give one child a large ball of colorful yarn. Have the child turn to his or her right-hand neighbor and make a warm, friendly comment. Tell the children you call such comments "fuzzies."[1]

The first time you have a *Fuzzy Comments* circle, the children will probably make simple statements, such as "I like you" or "You're nice."

1. The terms *warm fuzzies* and *cold pricklies* appear first in Alvyn Freed, *TA for Tots and Other Prinzes* (Sacramento, Calif.: Jalmar Press, 1973).

In succeeding circles, model and encourage statements of greater depth and variety. Call a child a good helper, for example, and confirm your statement by adding that you saw him or her help a classmate pick up crayons that fell on the floor.

# The Friendly Box

Tell the children that for a whole week they are going to keep track of all the friendly actions they do for one another. Explain that they will write a note about each friendly act and put the note into a box called *The Friendly Box*.

Then, have the children decorate a box with flowers, hearts, or animals and label it *The Friendly Box*. Cut a 1″ x 6″ slot in the top of the box. On the bottom of the box cut out a 4″ x 6″ rectangle and make a door out of it by reattaching the rectangle to one side of the opening with masking tape. For the latch, cut a 2″ x 3″ piece of cardboard and attach it with a paper fastener to the opposite side of the opening. Put *The Friendly Box* in a center supplied with 3″ x 5″ cards and pencils.

Begin the *Friendly Box* activity by gathering the children in a circle and reviewing ways to show friendliness. Have each child volunteer a way to be friendly or tell about a time when someone was friendly toward him or her. Point out the 3″ x 5″ cards and the pencils and explain that whenever a child experiences something friendly being done by a classmate, he or she should write the person's name and describe the friendly action on a 3″ x 5″ card and then slip the card into *The Friendly Box.* Have children who cannot print yet draw a picture to describe the friendly action or feeling experienced, or they can dictate their comments to you.

At the end of the day, form the *Friendly Box* circle. Open the door on the bottom of the box and remove the cards. Read each card aloud. Have the children share in the reading. Continue this project for one week. Each day the acts of friendliness will increase. By the end of the week, the box may overflow!

# Wheel of Friendly Acts

An alternate activity for encouraging friendly behavior is the *Wheel of Friendly Acts* circle.

Begin by asking the children to tell about things people have done for them that made them feel good or special. Print some of these ideas on a wheel similar to the one on this page. Make a tagboard arrow and attach it to the center of the wheel with a paper fastener. Have the children role play the friendly actions printed on the wheel.

Extend the activity by asking each child to decide how he or she is going to be friendly that day. If the children have difficulty deciding, suggest that they spin the activity wheel and try to do the action it suggests. Then have each child draw or write about the friendly action he or she plans to do that day.

During the *Wheel of Friendly Acts* circle at the end of the day, have the children share the friendly acts they did during the day and how they felt when they did them.

# Friend Commercials

Prepare for this activity by discussing with the children what a commercial is. Invite the children to share some of their favorite television commercials and to act them out.

Then divide the group into pairs and ask the partners to prepare commercials about each other. Tell them to describe nice things the partner does for others and why the partner would make a fabulous friend.

# Feelings and Values Circles

These ten activities develop children's self-understanding by helping them learn to identify feelings, to choose constructive ways to deal with their feelings, and to determine what they value.

## Microphone Stories

The concept circle is an excellent opportunity for the children to tell about actual experiences and to make up stories.

Gather the children into a circle and introduce the subject of feelings by asking each child to share a funny experience he or she has had. Point out that it is good to laugh at funny experiences but that poking fun at people can hurt their feelings.

Use an old tape recorder microphone or make a mike to use as the prop for this circle activity. (See page 94 for instructions on making a microphone.) Microphones increase fun and participation regardless of which concept or topic you are discussing, so use the microphone prop during other story-telling circles, too.

Limiting each child to a specific time increases the quality of the presentation and the concentration of the group. If the children are able to identify sentences, limit the comments to a specific number of sentences.

# Wishing on a Present

Feelings of longing and desire will emerge when children share gift wishes with one another.

The participation prop for this activity is a colorful gift box, wrapped so the children can still lift the box cover and peek inside.

Ask the children to think of something that they want more than anything else and that could be in the box. As each child slowly and gently shakes the present, he or she says,

> I wish, I wish my wish comes true;
> I shake the package for a clue.

Then he or she (and only the one whose turn it is) peeks to see if the wish came true.

Extend the wishing circle by asking the children to make up stories about the wished-for articles.

## Something Valuable

Valued articles give rise to good feelings, so ask each child to think of one thing that they value very, very much. Assign each child a day of the week on which he or she can bring the prized possession to school. (Inform parents a week in advance about this activity.) Suggest that children who are unable to bring a prized possession to school draw a picture of the article.

During a concept circle, have the children share how they feel about the prized possession and why it is so important to them.

## What's Important to Me

When children know what they consider important, they understand better their feelings about a subject and make wiser choices about the time and energy they expend on the subject.

During the *What's Important to Me* circle have the children talk about what is important to them.

Follow up the discussion by duplicating and passing out the page of pictures. Ask the children to think carefully about the things they do in school each day. Have each child cut the pictures out, arrange them in order from what is the least important to him or her to what is the most important. Then ask the children to paste the pictures in that order onto a second sheet of paper.

Return to the circle and ask the children to share why they ordered the pictures as they did.

# What Is Important to Me?

Art

Math

Writing

Social Studies

Reading

Music

abc Spelling

Physical Education

Science

# Stick Faces

Consider "stick faces" as an identification prop for children to use when they decide if their feelings on specific issues are happy or sad.

Have the children cut out two round circles from construction paper, color a happy face on one circle and a sad face on the other circle, and paste the circles back to back on the end of a popsicle stick.

During the *Stick Faces* circle, read the issues below and ask the children to share their feelings about the issues by turning their sticks either to the happy or to the sad face. Remind the children that there are *no* right or wrong answers.

Issues to raise are

- How do you feel when someone pushes you?
- How do you feel when someone smiles at you?
- How do you feel when the teacher calls on you?
- How do you feel about reading?
- How to you feel when no one plays with you?

- How do you feel when your best friend is sick?
- How do you feel when someone tells you that he or she likes you?
- How do you feel when it rains all day?
- How do you feel about pumpkin pie?
- How do you feel about riding in an airplane?
- How do you feel when your mom or dad is sick?
- How do you feel during the summer?
- How do you feel in the dark?
- How do you feel when someone gives you a gift?

# Feelings Thermometer

Children meet new experiences and repeat old ones daily. You can never be entirely certain of how each child will feel about a new experience. You can only guess on the basis of what you see. A *Feelings Thermometer* circle might help you in your guessing. What the children share during this circle may surprise you. You may discover that some of the events the children experience daily in their classroom life make them very sad or upset. By knowing which incidents lead to unhappiness, you can help the children convert these experiences to happy ones.

Give each child a precut 6" x 16" strip of tagboard. Have the children

draw on one end a picture of how they look when they are happy and on the other end a picture of how they look when they are sad. Ask the children to connect the two faces with a line and to divide the line into five equal parts with one-inch crossbars.

In the *Feelings Thermometer* circle, read aloud one of the following situation statements:

- Talking in front of the class makes me feel. . . .

- When I make things with my hands, I feel. . . .

- During reading, I feel. . . .

- During free time, I feel. . .

- When I come to school each morning, I feel. . . .

- Doing reports for class makes me feel. . . .

- When I share, I feel. . . .

- When my family visits the room, I feel. . . .

- During lunchtime, I feel. . . .

- Friends make me feel. . . .

- During music time, I feel. . . .

- When my teacher reads a story, I feel. . . .

- During recess, I feel. . . .

- When I get my papers back, I feel. . . .

- When I clean the room, I feel. . . .

- During spelling tests, I feel. . . .

Then ask the children to attach a paper clip by the crossbar that most closely represents how happy or how sad they think they would feel in that situation. Give each child an opportunity to show his or her thermometer to the class and to talk about his or her choice.

## Feeling Hats

Using special hats to identify feelings and having group members share times when they've had those feelings emphasizes for children the normalcy of experiencing a variety of feelings.

Pin the word *angry* to a hat. Have the children one by one put the hat on and tell about a time when they felt angry. In subsequent *Feeling Hats* circles, use the word *happy, lonely, sad, nervous,* or *afraid.*

# Feeling Masks

Masks help children project themselves into other roles and are especially useful for having children act out emotions they find difficult to explore or to cope with.

Trace the masks on pages 65-67 onto heavy tagboard. Cut out each mask, color it, and attach a popsicle stick to its neck.

During a *Feeling Masks* circle, have each child choose a mask, hold the mask in front of his or her face, and act out the emotion portrayed on the mask.

Extend the activity beyond the circle time by asking the children to work in pairs or groups of three and to write lines of dialog that verbalize the expressions on the masks.

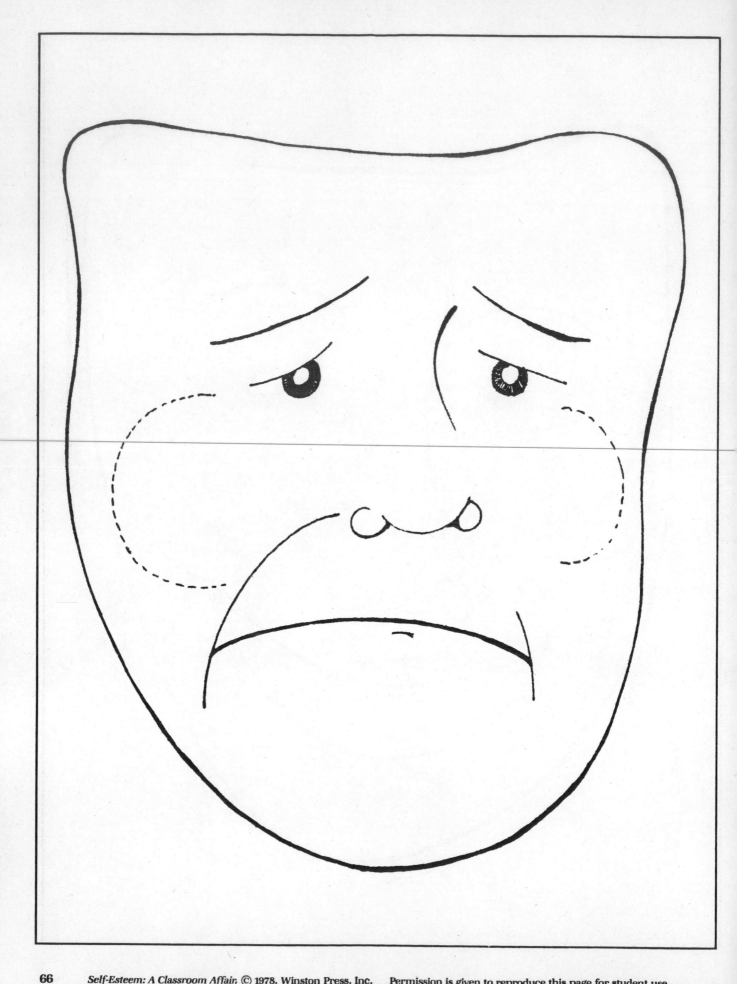

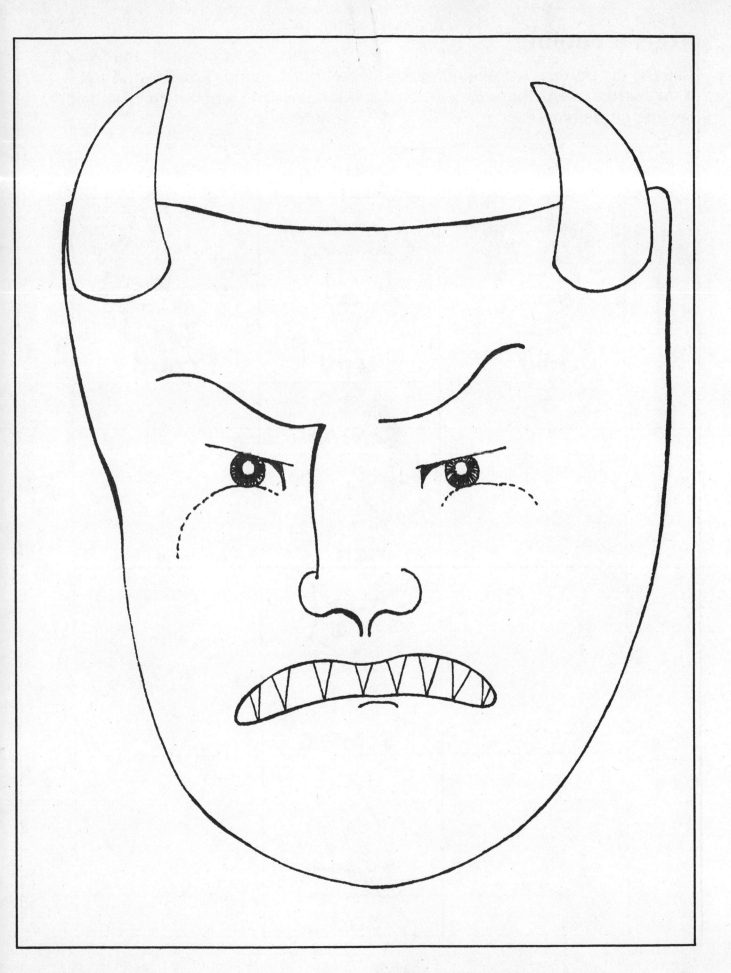

# Toss a Feeling

Use the die pattern below and make a tagboard die. During a *Toss-a-Feeling* circle have each child toss the die, think about the feeling word that lands faceup, and tell about a time when he or she had that feeling.

Paste

Silly

Happy

Proud

Mad

cut on dotted lines

Fold on solid lines

Scared

sad

 *Self-Esteem: A Classroom Affair*, © 1978, Winston Press, Inc.

# Feelings and Choices

This activity helps children recognize how their feelings affect their choices. Such an awareness frees children to make more responsible and just choices.

On 5" x 8" cards write the situation statements listed below.

- Somebody calls you a bad name.
- Nobody will play with you at recess.
- Your best friend broke his or her arm.
- You left your homework at home.
- The teacher asks you to talk in class.
- Your friend just pushed you down.
- Your lunch money is missing.
- Your friend told you that you did a nice job.
- You won first place in a race.
- Your bike has a flat tire.
- Your friend received a new toy and you didn't.
- Your teacher didn't choose you for the game.
- You had a nightmare last night.
- You have the chicken pox.
- You hear thunder.
- You are going to fly to Disneyland.
- It is Saturday.
- Your pet died.

- Your teacher said, "That's great!"
- You have to go to the dentist.
- You lost the game you played with a friend.

Gather the children in a *Feelings and Choices* circle. Place the cards in the center of the circle. Divide the group into pairs. Have each pair pick a card and read the situation statement. Then ask the pair to role play a response to the situation.

After the role play, ask the children to share the feelings they had during the role play and to discuss how those feelings influenced their choices and actions.

# Award Circles

Use the following award circles to announce success and to stimulate feelings of worth and self-esteem.

## Buddy Award

Before having a *Buddy Award* circle, duplicate the award button on this page. Duplicate enough buttons so you can give one to each child in your classroom.

Begin the *Buddy Award* circle in the morning by describing the Buddy Award. (See also the *Secret Buddies* activity on page 57.) Have each child share one way in which a person can be a buddy.

At the end of the day, continue the *Buddy Award* circle by having the children tell about classmates who were extra special buddies that day. Write the names of these buddies on the awards and present the *Buddy Award* to the successful children. Suggest that the recipients take them home and proudly display them.

Encourage continued buddy behavior by announcing that one day soon you will conduct another *Buddy Award* circle.

Before introducing the *Royalty-Award* circle, make a tinfoil crown or purchase one in a variety store.

Then gather the children in a circle and explain that each time they have this concept circle, one child will be king or queen for the day. During the *Royalty-Award* circle, have the king or queen you have chosen wear the crown and sit regally on his or her throne while the other children take turns making kind comments about the royal person. Record the student comments on an affidavit of royalty similar to the one illustrated here and suggest that the child proudly take the award home.

Choose the king or queen of the day by rotation. Post the list of future royalty to increase anticipation of the happy event.

# Royalty Award

Erin is our friend. We like him and he likes us.
Erin says so many nice, warm, fuzzy things.
He likes to play with blocks. Erin's smile makes
us feel good. We're glad Erin is in our class.

Prepared by the students of _____
(class)

Recorded by _____
(teacher)

at _____
(school)

Date _____

The *Happy-Day-Feelings Award* circle meets as a finale to the school day. Have each child describe something that made his or her day a happy one; for example, that a friend's action made him or her feel special or that doing a good job on a project made him or her feel capable. Have a duplicated *Happy-Day-Feelings-Award* button available for each child. After each child shares a happy experience during the *Happy-Day-Feelings-Award* circle, write his or her name on a button and give it to the child. Remember to comment on the good feelings you have when your students talk about their happy feelings.

*Self-Esteem: A Classroom Affair,* © 1978, Winston Press, Inc.   Permission is given to reproduce this page for student use.

# Chapter Six

# Puppets...Puppets...Puppets

A child's world is fresh and new and beautiful, full of wonder and excitement.

Rachel L. Carson
*The Sense of Wonder*

# Using Puppets

Children adore puppets. Use the fantasy world of puppet activities to help children identify emotions, increase self-awareness, and develop self-confidence. When the children use puppets to project themselves into the character of another person, they find that it is easier to role play that person's feelings. Often the children will also feel freer to talk about the feelings they projected.

Shy children derive particular benefit from using puppets. Somehow when they manipulate the puppets and make them talk, their self-confidence jumps sky high.

Give children the opportunity to play with the puppets alone, in small groups, or in concept circles.

# Finger Puppets

Finger puppets have the advantage of being small and quick to make. They slip easily into a pocket, ready to be drawn out at the snap of a finger in order to entertain oneself or a friend.

Encourage the children to pretend the puppets are make-believe characters as well as family and friends.

## Ring Puppets

Cut a strip of paper 2½″ x 1″. Overlap and paste the ends together to make a ring. Cut out circles the size of a quarter and draw a face in each circle. Paste a face onto each ring, slip the ring on your finger, and you're ready to role play or fantasize.

## Glove Puppets

Cut off the fingers of an old glove about 2½″ from the fingertips. Using fine felt-tip pens, draw the face of a favorite person or story-book character on each cloth finger. Slip a glove puppet on your finger and pretend you are that character.

Put on two finger puppets (either on a single hand or one on each hand) and have these puppets carry on a conversation. Remind the children to change their voices for each character.

## Paper Puppets

Duplicate the puppets on the next page on heavy tagboard or construction paper. Have the children complete the plain puppet. Suggest that they may want to make self-puppets so they can be part of the situations they will act out later on with their puppets. Cut out the puppet's hands (the two holes in the center of each puppet). Have the children put their index and middle fingers through these holes, and then watch the fun begin.

Now, ask the children to pretend that these puppets are friends and to act out friendship situations with them. Possible situations are

• Your next-door neighbor cut his or her finger on a piece of glass.

• You know it's a classmate's birthday.

• A classmate has a broken arm and can't play catch with your group.

• You want to tell someone about your new pet.

• Your sister/brother is crying, and you want to show you care.

# Paper-Bag Puppets

Use puppetry as a technique for building self-awareness. Have each child make a puppet of him or herself and use the puppet during a concept circle to express his or her own opinions.

Pass around old hand mirrors and give the children time to study their facial features well. Provide each child with a marked, construction paper outline of a face and with color crayons. Ask the children to make puppet look-alikes. Have the children work in pairs. Ask them to make sure their partners use the appropriate colors for skin, hair, and eyes.

When the look-alikes are complete, have each child cut the face out of the construction paper and then cut the face along the broken lines. Give each child a paper bag. (Provide paper bags small enough so the children can manipulate them easily.) Tell the children to paste the upper part of the face onto the bottom flap of the bag and the chin onto the side of the bag immediately under the bottom flap. When the bag is folded flat, the chin should match up with the rest of the face.

**Family puppets.** Extend this puppet activity by having the children create paper-bag puppets with the likeness of each member of their family and also of their friends. Creating plays with the larger repertoire of puppets helps children increase their awareness of the feelings and thoughts of other people and of other age groups.

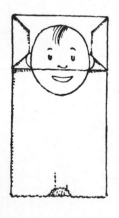

# Felt Puppets

Felt puppets are soft and flexible props for children to use when telling stories or for acting out feelings.

## Materials Needed
- two flesh-colored 8″ x 11″ pieces of felt
- puppet template
- 8″ x 11″ cardboard or tagboard
- large-eye needles
- #10 sewing thread
- fabric and yarn remnants
- buttons, lace, sequins, ribbons, glitter
- sewing machine (optional)

Have each child bring two 8″ x 11″ flesh-colored pieces of felt from home. (Have some on hand for those who forget or are unable to purchase them.)

Make a cardboard or tagboard template from the outline on this page. Help the children trace the puppet pattern onto their pieces of felt. Then, have each child cut out the two pattern pieces and whipstitch them together. Remind the children to leave the bottom edge of the puppet open. (A parent helper can assist with this project by bringing a sewing machine to the classroom and machine stitching the puppets for the children.)

Suggest that the children dress the puppets with fabric clothes. (The broken lines on the pattern indicate the area to be traced for the clothes.) Glue or sew on yarn hair and button eyes. Embroider the mouth. Lace, sequins, ribbons, and glitter make good trim material and add to the puppets' finished look.

# Unpuppets

Felt puppets are also very effective left faceless and unadorned. Use pieces of felt in a variety of colors. Follow the directions on page 77 for tracing, cutting, and sewing felt puppets. Cut out and attach a piece of flesh-colored felt for the face but give the puppets no facial features.

Unpuppets work well in concept circles about feelings. Write several feelings or feeling situations on cards and put the cards in a hat. Pass the hat around the circle and have each child use an unpuppet to portray the feeling or situation called for on the card he or she pulls from the hat. Because the puppets are faceless, the children need to rely strongly on puppet gestures and verbalizations.

# Stick Puppets

See *Talking Box* activity 1, page 81, for a further puppet variation—making Stick Puppets.

# Puppet Stage

Children have great fun putting on puppet plays on a puppet stage. They enjoy being able to hide behind the curtains, move their puppets about on the stage, and mimic the characters' voices.

Build a simple stage out of a good-sized, rectangular cardboard box. Remove one of the larger sides completely. Cut a large opening on the opposite side for the stage front. Glue or staple stage curtains to the inside of the stage opening. Place the stage on a table to which you've attached a table skirt. The puppeteers can then remain invisible to their audience.

# Chapter Seven

# The Talking Box Project

Love and self-worth are so intertwined that they may properly be related through the use of the term *identity.* Thus we may say that the single basic need that people have is the requirement for an identity: the belief that we are someone in distinction to others and that the someone is important and worthwhile. Then love and self-worth may be considered the two pathways that mankind has discovered lead to a successful identity.

William Glasser
*Schools Without Failure*

## The Talking Box Project

Self-confidence is the basic ingredient necessary for feeling secure enough to participate in group language activities. Children with low self-esteem require a variety of positive experiences before they feel confident in a group language activity.

When one of our students is reticent about speaking in front of the class, we try to involve him or her in small-group talking experiences, beginning with one-to-one peer conversations. As confidence increases, we gradually increase the difficulty and complexity of the tasks and extend the talking activities to small groups of children. Eventually the child begins to volunteer during large-group talking activities.

This chapter provides activities that ask children to practice language skills—skills that will increase a child's self-confidence. Directions are given below for making a box that will house the activities. Set up the *Talking Box* in the activity center. The materials for each activity are contained in envelopes—there are fifteen in all—on which directions to the children about a talking activity are printed. Materials for some of the activities will not fit into the envelopes. These materials should be placed near the *Talking Box*.

Before introducing this project, make the *Talking Box*, collect or make the materials to be used in the fifteen activities (pages 81-96), and duplicate a *Talking Box* contract (page 97) for each child in the room. The contract will become a checklist that shows which activities a child has completed.

When you introduce the project to the children, show them the *Talking Box* and its contents and explain its use. (Tell the children that they do not need to do the activities in order.) Then show the children some of the materials in the various envelopes and point out the additional materials in the activity center. Tell the children when they can use the *Talking Box*.

Next, give each child a contract and explain its use. Ask the children to write their names on the contracts and tell them where the contracts will be kept.

Finally, show the children the *Talking Box* certificate (page 98) and promise them that you will give them a certificate after they finish the fifteen activities.

**Materials Needed for the *Talking Box***
- large box
- fifteen 9″ x 12″ envelopes
- construction paper
- paper for decorating box
- decorating motif
- paste or glue
- scissors
- felt-tip marker
- duplicated contracts (one per child)
- duplicated certificates (one per child)

**Making the *Talking Box*.** Obtain a box large enough to hold fifteen 9″ x 12″ activity envelopes filled with activity props or other materials.

First, cover the box with plain background paper. Then, decorate the box with a motif, such as butterflies, inchworms, flowers, or frogs. Make a pattern and trace the motif on construction paper. If the children help you prepare this project, have them cut out the motifs and paste or glue them onto the box. Use the same motif for the *Talking Box* contract and certificate. (The reproducible samples use a butterfly motif.)

**Making the *Talking Box* activity envelopes.** Write the directions for each of the fifteen *Talking Box* activities on separate 9″ x 12″ envelopes. Or duplicate the fifteen sets of directions and paste each set on a separate envelope.

Code the upper right-hand corner of each envelope with the project motif and the number of that activity. Put the appropriate activity props and materials into each envelope. Place large or heavy materials in the activity center.

**Making the *Talking Box* contract.** Duplicate a *Talking Box* contract for each child (page 97). Or create your own contract using the same motif with which you identified the activity envelopes and decorated the *Talking Box* itself.

# The Talking Box Activities

On the front of the first *Talking Box* activity envelope, put the following set of directions, which give the children the opportunity to present a puppet play.

**Materials Needed**
- magazines
- popsicle sticks
- two scissors
- paste or glue

Put a large number of popsicle sticks in the activity envelope. (You will have to replenish these frequently.) Put the magazines, paste, and scissors in the activity center.

## Make Up Stick-Puppet Plays

1. Choose a partner.
2. Take out some magazines and find pictures of four faces.
3. Take four popsicle sticks out of this envelope.
4. Cut out one face for each popsicle stick.
5. Paste the face on the end of a popsicle stick. (You've made a puppet!)
6. Make up a puppet play and present it to the class.
7. Put away the magazines, paste, and scissors.
8. Get your *Talking Box* contracts. Color picture number one.
9. Take your puppets home and give a puppet play for your family.

# Feel Something and Tell About It

1. Choose a partner.
2. Find the Feely Bag.
3. Take the blindfold out of this envelope and put it on.
4. Put your hand into the bag and feel one of the things in the bag.
5. Tell your partner five things about how the thing feels.
6. See if you and your partner can guess what the thing is.
7. Give your partner a turn.
8. Now, take turns and tell about two more things.
9. Put the Feely Bag away and put the blindfold back in the activity envelope.
10. Get your *Talking Box* contracts. Color picture number two.

On the front of the second *Talking Box* activity envelope, put the directions which give children the opportunity to describe something in the Feely Bag.

**Materials Needed**
- a Feely Bag        • a blindfold
- several small objects, such as a sponge, bar of soap, rope, ruler, pencil, penny, button, toy car, plastic animal, cotton ball, ring, nail clipper, plastic flower, sock, block of wood, clothespin

Use a paper bag or sew a bag from fabric. Use a shoelace or piece of cord for a drawstring. Make sure the Feely Bag is a dark color so the children cannot see the objects in it.

Try one of the following ideas for making a blindfold:

- Cover the eye holes of a Halloween mask with tape.
- Use a sleeping mask.
- Use a large paper bag.
- Cut out two layers of felt in the shape of a sleeping mask. Whipstitch the edges of the felt together. Attach the ends of a single piece of elastic to the sides of the mask.

Place the blindfold in the activity envelope. Put the small articles you've collected into the Feely Bag; keep the bag in the activity center. Be sure to point out the Feely Bag to the children when you introduce the *Talking Box* project.

# Ask Questions

1. Choose a partner.
2. Pretend that you are a newspaper reporter and that you go around town asking people questions. Today, you want to learn what school children think and how they feel.
3. Take one question card out of this envelope.
4. Ask your partner the question on the card.
5. Pick out two more cards. Ask your partner these questions.
6. Have your partner ask you three questions.
7. Put the question cards back in the activity envelope.
8. Get your *Talking Box* contracts. Color picture number three.

On the front of the third *Talking Box* activity envelope, put the directions which give the children the opportunity to ask interview questions.

**Materials Needed**
- 3" x 5" cards
- a felt-tip pen

**Making question cards.** Print interview questions on 3" x 5" cards. Consider using the following interview questions:
- What are some favorite things you do?
- What are your favorite movies?
- What makes a good friend?
- What makes you happy?
- What makes you angry?
- What makes you sad?
- What do you like about school?
- What do you want to change at school?
- Why should children go to school?
- What does your house look like?
- What do you like about your home?
- What do you want to change about your home?

Put the question cards in the activity envelope.

# Tell Silly Stories

1. Choose a partner.
2. Find the *Book of Silly Faces.*
3. Take the Story Wheel out of this envelope.
4. Flip the pages of the *Book of Silly Faces* and make a silly face.
5. Tell your partner a silly story about this silly face. Use the Story Wheel for ideas. Spin the Story Wheel arrow four times. The arrow will point to a question about the face you made. Make the answers part of your story.
6. Give your partner a turn.
7. Now, take turns making two more silly faces and telling silly stories about them.
8. Put the *Book of Silly Faces* away and put the Story Wheel back in the activity envelope.
9. Get your *Talking Box* contracts. Color picture number four.

On the front of the fourth *Talking Box* activity envelope, put the directions which give the children an opportunity to tell silly stories.

## Materials Needed
- magazines
- 8½" x 11" construction paper
- paste or glue
- scissors
- pencils
- a paper punch
- an 8½" x 11" three-ring binder
- an 8" square of tagboard
- tagboard for arrow
- a paper fastener

**Making the *Book of Silly Faces.*** Have the children help you look through old magazines to find pictures of faces large enough to fill 8½" x 11" sheets of paper. Paste or glue these pictures to sheets of construction paper. Punch three holes at the left-hand side of each picture. (Be sure to match the holes to the rings in your binder.) Then mark and cut each page into three equal horizontal strips. Place the pictures in a binder entitled the *Book of Silly Faces.*

 *Self-Esteem: A Classroom Affair,* © 1978, Winston Press, Inc.

**Making the Story Wheel.** With a felt-tip marker, draw a circle on the 8″ tagboard, divide it into eight pie-shaped sections, and cut out the circle. Write one of the following questions in each section:

- Where does he or she work?
- How does he or she travel to a party?
- What does he or she like to do?
- Where does he or she live?
- What does he or she eat?
- What does he or she wear?
- What are his or her friends like?
- Does he or she have any pets?

With a paper fastener, attach a colorful tagboard arrow to the circle.

Put the Story Wheel in the activity envelope. Place the *Book of Silly Faces* in the activity center. Be sure the children know how to use the *Book of Silly Faces* before they begin the *Talking Box* project.

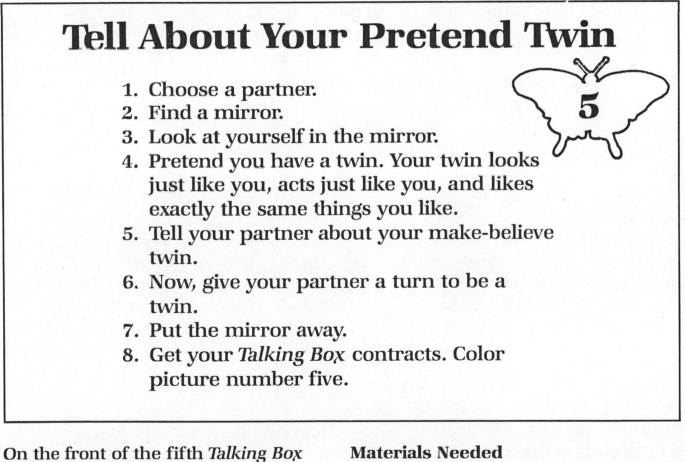

# Tell About Your Pretend Twin

1. Choose a partner.
2. Find a mirror.
3. Look at yourself in the mirror.
4. Pretend you have a twin. Your twin looks just like you, acts just like you, and likes exactly the same things you like.
5. Tell your partner about your make-believe twin.
6. Now, give your partner a turn to be a twin.
7. Put the mirror away.
8. Get your *Talking Box* contracts. Color picture number five.

On the front of the fifth *Talking Box* activity envelope, put the directions which give the children the opportunity to tell about themselves.

**Materials Needed**
- mirror

Put a mirror in the activity center.

# Answer Questions About Pictures

6

1. Choose a partner.
2. Take one picture out of this envelope.
   Look at it carefully.
3. Have your partner take three question cards out of this envelope and ask you the questions on the cards.
4. Look at the picture and answer the questions.
5. Have your partner look at a new picture while you ask three questions about it.
6. Now, take turns answering questions about one more picture.
7. Put the pictures and the question cards back in the activity envelope.
8. Get your *Talking Box* contracts. Color picture number six.

On the front of the sixth *Talking Box* activity envelope, put the directions which give the children an opportunity to express their feelings and opinions about pictures.

**Materials Needed**
- pictures on different themes
- construction paper or tagboard
- 3" x 5" cards
- paste or glue
- scissors
- a felt-tip marker

**Making the pictures.** From magazines, books, and calendars, cut out pictures on a variety of themes. Mount the pictures on construction paper or tagboard. Limit the size of the pictures so they will fit into the 9" x 12" activity envelope.

**Making the question cards.** On 3" x 5" cards, print the following questions:

- How do you feel when you look at this picture?

- How do the colors in the picture make you feel?
- What time of day do you think it is in this picture?
- What is this picture about?
- What title would you give this picture?
- Do you like this picture? Why?

- Is this picture about the way things are today? How do you know?

Put the question cards and the pictures in the activity envelope.

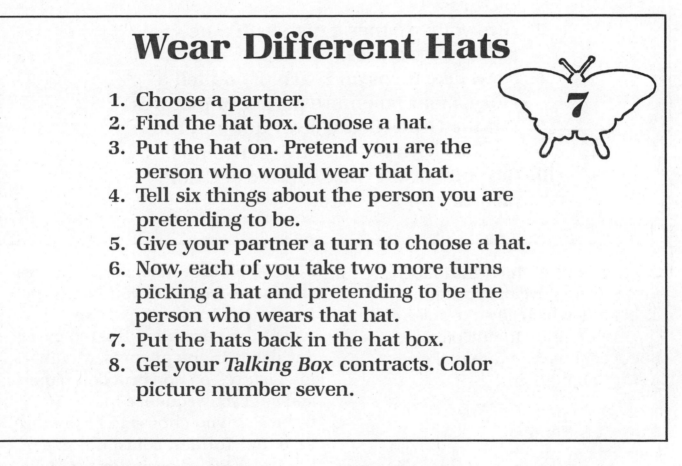

# Wear Different Hats

1. Choose a partner.
2. Find the hat box. Choose a hat.
3. Put the hat on. Pretend you are the person who would wear that hat.
4. Tell six things about the person you are pretending to be.
5. Give your partner a turn to choose a hat.
6. Now, each of you take two more turns picking a hat and pretending to be the person who wears that hat.
7. Put the hats back in the hat box.
8. Get your *Talking Box* contracts. Color picture number seven.

On the front of the seventh *Talking Box* activity envelope, put the directions which give the children an opportunity to role play.

**Materials Needed**
- many hats
- a box

**Collecting the hats.** Send home a request for old hats, especially those that suggest an occupation. Put the hats in a box, mark the box *HATS*, and place the box in the activity center.

# Tell Stories from the Pictures

1. Choose a partner.
2. Find the Order Board.
3. Take one packet out of this envelope.
4. Take the pictures out of the packet.
5. Look carefully at each picture. Put the pictures in the right order on the Order Board.
6. Tell your partner a story to go with the pictures.
7. Give your partner a turn with a new packet of pictures.
8. Now, take turns and each of you tell a story about one more packet of pictures.
9. Put the Order Board away and put the packets back in the activity envelope.
10. Get your *Talking Box* contracts. Color picture number eight.

On the front of the eighth *Talking Box* activity envelope, put the directions which give the children the opportunity to put pictures into a sequence and to make a story about them.

**Materials Needed**
- six sets of pictures, each of which tells a story
- correction fluid
- construction paper
- paste or glue
- scissors
- six small packets
- 8" x 18" tagboard
- stapler

**Making picture sets.** Select picture sequences from old workbooks or newspaper comic strips. Use typewriter correction fluid to cover any dialog in the pictures. Mount the pictures on construction paper and cut each sequence into four frames. (If you choose to have more than four frames, adjust the size of the Order Board accordingly.) Make six different picture sets and put each set into a small packet.

On each story envelope, print the following sentences:

- Put the pictures back carefully, please!
- Are there four pictures in this packet?

**Making an Order Board.** To make an Order Board on which the children can arrange the pictures, cut out an 8″ x 18″ piece of tagboard, fold up 1½″ on the bottom edge, and staple the folded section at 4½″ intervals to create pockets for the pictures.

Put the six packets containing the picture sets into the activity envelope. Place the Order Board in the activity center. Explain the use of the Order Board when you introduce the *Talking Box* project.

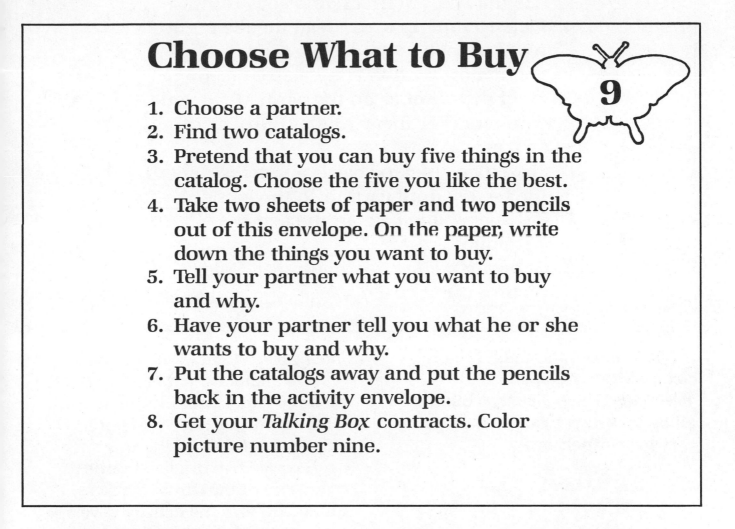

# Choose What to Buy

**9**

1. Choose a partner.
2. Find two catalogs.
3. Pretend that you can buy five things in the catalog. Choose the five you like the best.
4. Take two sheets of paper and two pencils out of this envelope. On the paper, write down the things you want to buy.
5. Tell your partner what you want to buy and why.
6. Have your partner tell you what he or she wants to buy and why.
7. Put the catalogs away and put the pencils back in the activity envelope.
8. Get your *Talking Box* contracts. Color picture number nine.

On the front of the ninth *Talking Box* activity envelope, put the directions which give the children the opportunity to make choices and to verbalize why they chose as they did.

**Materials Needed**
• two catalogs
• writing paper (one piece for each child in the classroom)
• two pencils

Put the writing paper and the pencils in the activity envelope. Find two catalogs that contain things of interest to children and put them in the activity center.

# Play a Game About Feelings

10

1. Choose a partner.
2. Take everything out of this envelope.
3. Shuffle the cards. Put the cards face down on the game board. Whoever has the shorter first name goes first.
4. Pick up the top card. Read the feeling word or look at the feeling picture. Tell about a time when you had that feeling.
5. Read the number on the card. Move your game marker forward that number of spaces.
6. Take turns picking cards and telling about the feeling until you finish the game.
7. Put everything back in the activity envelope.
8. Get your *Talking Box* contracts. Color picture number ten.

On the front of the tenth *Talking Box* activity envelope, put the directions which give the children an opportunity to share feelings they have experienced.

**Materials Needed**
- 8½" x 11" tagboard
- two markers
- pictures depicting feelings
- a rubber band
- paper
- 3" x 5" cards

**Preparing the materials.** Make a game board like the one opposite.

On 3" x 5" cards to which you have assigned a number value from one to three, write feeling words, such as *angry, happy, shy, excited,* *lonely, scared, silly, grouchy, sad.*

On additional cards, mount pictures that express feelings. Stack all the cards together and put a rubber band around them.

Provide two different game markers. Put the cards, markers, and board into the activity envelope.

Tell about a time when you felt...

Put your game cards here.

Start

# Describe a Friend

**11**

1. Choose a partner.
2. Find a timer.
3. Take a piece of paper and a pencil out of this envelope.
4. Sit down and look carefully at your partner. Think of ways to describe your partner.
5. Set the timer for one minute. Have your partner make a mark on the paper each time you name something about him or her. Name as many things as you can in one minute.
6. Give your partner a chance to describe you.
7. Now, take turns describing two other classmates.
8. Put the timer away and put the pencil back in the activity envelope.
9. Get your *Talking Box* contracts. Color picture number eleven.

On the front of the eleventh *Talking Box* activity envelope, put the directions which give the children the opportunity to describe a friend.

**Materials Needed**
- a timer
- paper (one piece for each child in the classroom)
- a pencil

Put the pencil and the paper in the activity envelope. Put the timer in the activity center. Explain its use, if the children are unfamiliar with timers.

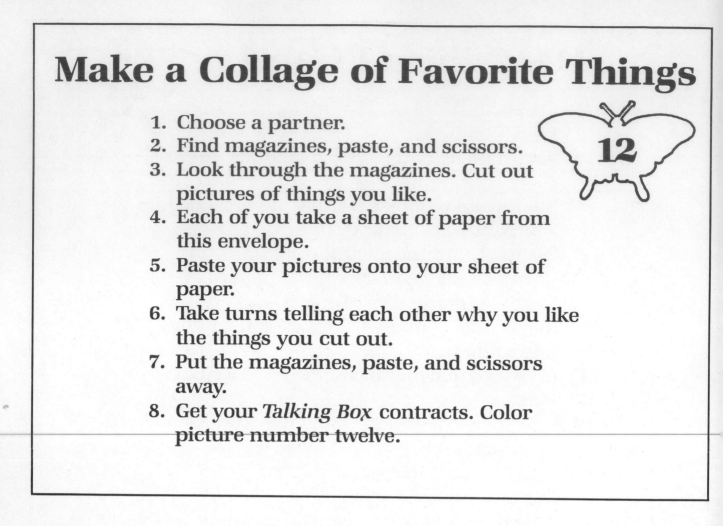

# Make a Collage of Favorite Things

1. Choose a partner.
2. Find magazines, paste, and scissors.
3. Look through the magazines. Cut out pictures of things you like.
4. Each of you take a sheet of paper from this envelope.
5. Paste your pictures onto your sheet of paper.
6. Take turns telling each other why you like the things you cut out.
7. Put the magazines, paste, and scissors away.
8. Get your *Talking Box* contracts. Color picture number twelve.

12

On the front of the twelfth *Talking Box* activity envelope, put the directions which give the children the opportunity to make a collage of their favorite things and to tell why they like these things.

**Materials Needed**
- magazines
- construction paper (one sheet for each child in the classroom)
- paste or glue
- scissors

Put the construction paper in the activity envelope. Place the magazines, paste, and scissors in the activity center.

# Make Up Matching Sets

1. Choose a partner.
2. Find the box marked *SETS*. Take several things out of the box. Find things that are alike and make a set out of them.
3. Tell your partner how the things are alike.
4. Give your partner a turn.
5. Now, take turns and each of you make five more sets.
6. Put your sets of things back in the box marked *SETS*.
7. Get your *Talking Box* contracts. Color picture number thirteen.

**13**

On the front of the thirteenth *Talking Box* activity envelope, put the directions which give the children the opportunity to make sets of similar things and to tell how they are alike.

**Materials Needed**
- a box
- articles, such as sponge, soap, safety pin, pencil, ruler, clothespin, paper, block, plastic fruit, toy car, toy boat, toy plane, play animals, eraser, chalk, seeds, jewelry, paper bag, bell, pen, pair of glasses, doll furniture, comb, cooking utensils, rubber band, paper clip, doll clothes, buttons, nails, screws and nuts, playing cards, macaroni, rice, raisin box, oatmeal box, cracker box, flour bag, sugar bag

Put all the articles into a box. Print the word *SETS* on the box. Place the box in the activity center.

Since the concept of sets may be difficult for the children, introduce the concept before you begin the *Talking Box* project. Give examples of ways in which articles are similar and part of a set. For example: show that a toy car could be part of a set of toys, of a set of cars, or of a set of things that had lights or windows or doors.

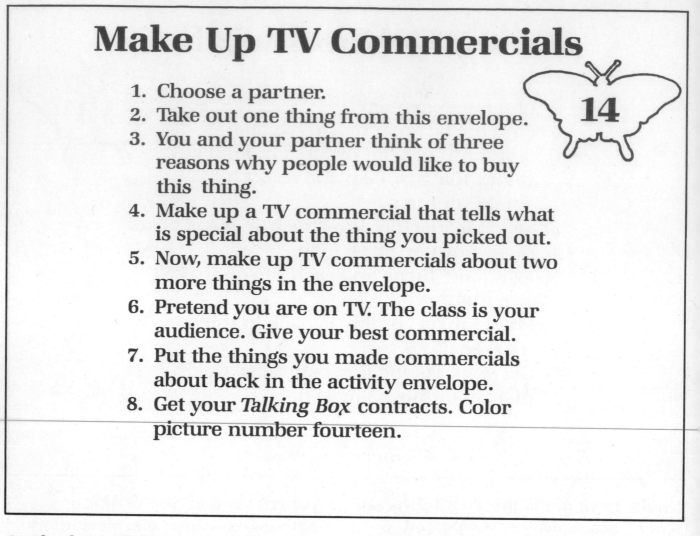

# Make Up TV Commercials

1. Choose a partner.
2. Take out one thing from this envelope.
3. You and your partner think of three reasons why people would like to buy this thing.
4. Make up a TV commercial that tells what is special about the thing you picked out.
5. Now, make up TV commercials about two more things in the envelope.
6. Pretend you are on TV. The class is your audience. Give your best commercial.
7. Put the things you made commercials about back in the activity envelope.
8. Get your *Talking Box* contracts. Color picture number fourteen.

**14**

On the front of the fourteenth *Talking Box* activity envelope, put the directions which give the children the opportunity to think up TV commercials and present them to their classmates.

## Materials Needed
- bar of soap
- band-aid
- pepper or salt wrapped in cellophane
- gum wrapper
- raisin box
- pencil
- color crayon
- tooth brush
- checker piece
- marble
- chalk

Put the props for making up TV commercials in the activity envelope.

**Making a microphone.** Children might enjoy using a microphone when they give their commercials. To make a mike, obtain a tube from a roll of paper toweling. Crumple some paper into a ball and use it for the microphone speaker. For the microphone cord, anchor a 3' piece of rug yarn in the paper ball and thread the unanchored end through the tube. Cover the tube and the paper ball with tinfoil. (Or you may want to use an old tape-recorder microphone as the prop.)

# Make Telephone Calls

1. Choose a partner.
2. Find two play telephones.
3. Take out the red and the yellow cards from this envelope.
4. Read one red card. Decide whom to call for help.
5. Look through the yellow cards and find the number you want to call.
6. Carefully dial the telephone number.
7. Have your partner answer your call. Tell your partner who you are and why you are calling.
8. When you finish your call, remember to say "thank you" and "good-bye" before replacing the receiver.
9. Have your partner pick a red card and make a call.
10. Now, take turns solving two more problems.
11. Put the telephones away and the cards back in the activity envelope.
12. Get your *Talking Box* contracts. Color picture number fifteen.

On the front of the fifteenth *Talking Box* activity envelope, put the directions which give the children an opportunity to make telephone calls.

**Materials Needed**
- two play telephones
- red and yellow 3" x 5" construction-paper cards

Before introducing the *Talking Box* project to the children, teach them about the help they can receive when they dial the telephone operator and information. Explain dial tone, busy signal, and the need to let the telephone ring long enough for a person to answer it.

Prepare telephone-number cards that contain the names and

numbers required for this activity. Among these numbers should be that of the operator, information, emergency, the fire department, the police, a pizza parlor, and a movie theater. Put these names and numbers on yellow construction-paper cards.

Compose a list of tasks that identify problems the children can solve by calling an appropriate person. Write these tasks on red construction-paper cards. Use problems such as the following:

- You are sick and you need a doctor.

- Your house is on fire.

- There is a hippopotamus in your backyard.

- Your cat is stuck in a tree.

- A friend fell and broke his or her arm.

- You want to know what time a movie starts.

- Your partner left his or her homework at your house.

- Your parents ask you to order a pizza for supper.

Put the task cards and the telephone-number cards in the activity envelope. Place the telephones in the activity center.

# The Talking Box Contracts and Certificates

Create contracts and certificates using the same motif that you selected for decorating the *Talking Box*. Provide each child with a personal contract on which to record his or her language skill activity. This contract will serve as a checklist to help the children know which activities they have completed.

Trace the *Talking Box* motif on a sheet of paper fifteen times, number the motifs, and duplicate the contract on construction paper. Or duplicate the contract that appears on page 97.

As the children complete a language activity, have them color the motif that corresponds to the number of the activity just completed. Provide a place for the children to keep their contracts. Point the place out to the children when you introduce the *Talking Box* project.

When a child completes his or her contract sheet, give him or her a *Talking Box* certificate (page 98). Encourage the child to take the certificate home and show it proudly to family, neighbors, and friends.

# My *Talking Box* Contract

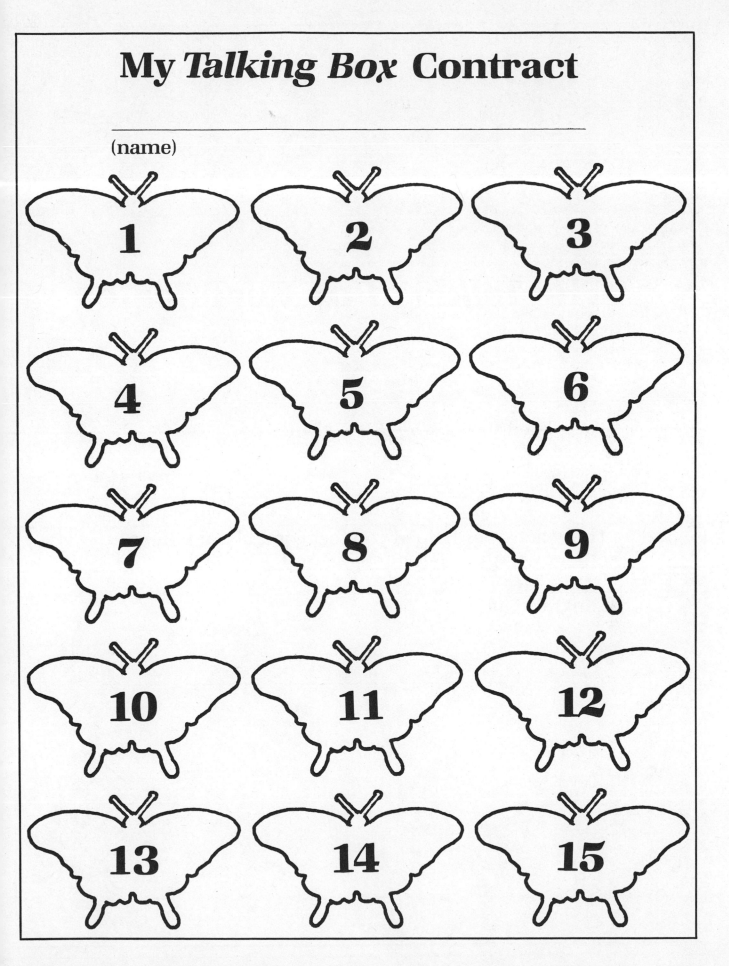

(name)

# The *Talking Box* Certificate

_____, you

completed the *Talking Box* activities on

_____

These activities helped you feel good about telling
others what you felt, thought, and wanted.

Congratulations!

signed _____

# Chapter Eight

# Helping Children See Their Progress

Over time, a continuing and steadfast focus on the positive in life, on our strengths, and on the strengths of others can help to restore in our students their personal energy, their feelings of power, their sense of self-worth so that they can see themselves as positive forces who can contribute to the task of building a better world.

Isabel L. Hawley
Robert C. Hawley
*Human Values in the Classroom*

# Encourage Realistic Progress

A number of years ago the psychologist Arthur T. Jersild pointed out that individuals with negative self-concepts make unrealistically high demands of themselves and are also unable to evaluate themselves accurately. Both characteristics raise the risk of failure. The sense of worthlessness that accompanies the failure confirms and increases the existing negative self-concept.

The activities in the first section of this chapter help children set realistic goals. The second set of activities help the children learn to evaluate themselves accurately by recording feelings and progress toward chosen goals. The final section of the chapter suggests some children's awards that will affirm their sense of accomplishment and self-worth.

# Set Goals

The chart on this page will help children focus on a single goal and keep track of how well they achieve that goal in a given day. The goals may be selected by the children or suggested by you.

Praise the children for any effort or achievement. Remembering just once to act a certain way or to work on a chosen activity may be a tremendous achievement in independence and responsibility for some children.

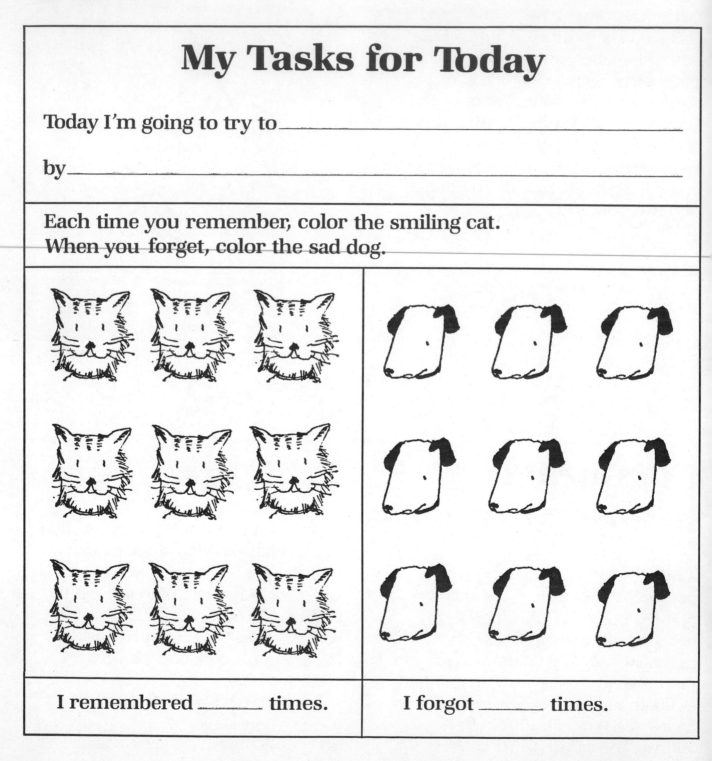

## My Tasks for Today

Today I'm going to try to _____

by _____

Each time you remember, color the smiling cat.
When you forget, color the sad dog.

I remembered _____ times.

I forgot _____ times.

Weekly goals are appropriate for tasks that require skill development. Individual learning differences are also better accommodated by allowing a longer time span for goal achievement.

Duplicate the chart below and have the children write their goals on the numbered lines.

# My Goals for This Week

by _____

1. _____

2. _____

3. _____

4. _____

5. _____

Next week I need to _____

_____

In each target, have the children print one goal they are going to pursue during the week. (Write for the children if necessary or more practical but involve them in choosing the goals.)

At the end of the week, ask the children how many targets they hit; that is, which goals they reached. If a child partially achieved the goal, allow him or her to claim half of the score. Then add up and help the children record their scores.

Suggest that the children color the targets that name goals they achieved. For partially achieved goals, suggest that the child color the outer ring of the target.

# My Targets for This Week

by _____

My score for this week is_____.

# Keep Records

## Academic Progress Charts

Charts are another way for children to record their performance. Adapt the examples shown below to fit your classroom activities.

In a central file, maintain folders for each child's progress charts. Remember to give children the opportunity to record their progress.

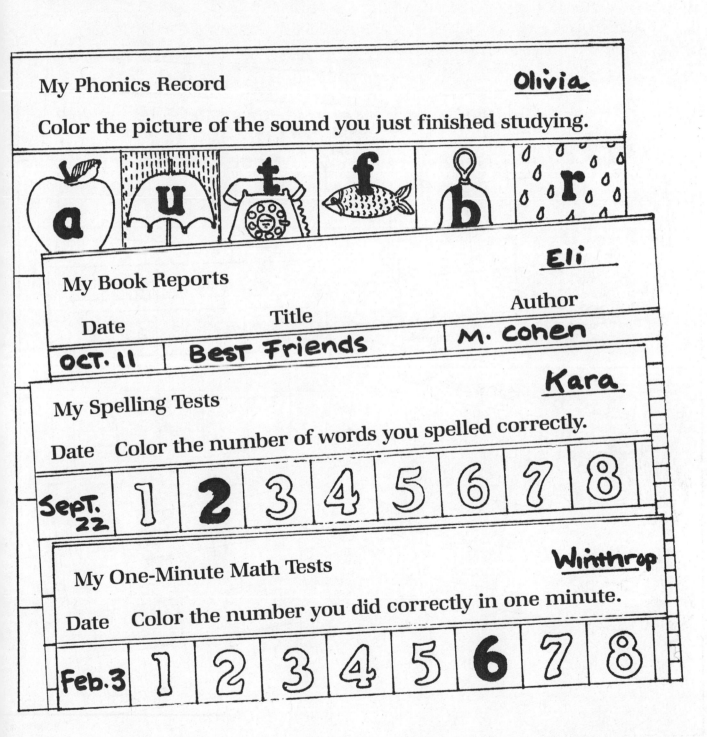

My Phonics Record          Olivia

Color the picture of the sound you just finished studying.

a  u  t  f  b  r

My Book Reports          Eli

| Date | Title | Author |
|------|-------|--------|
| OCT. 11 | BesT Friends | M. Cohen |

My Spelling Tests          Kara

Date   Color the number of words you spelled correctly.

| Date | | | | | | | | |
|------|--|--|--|--|--|--|--|--|
| Sept. 22 | 1 | 2 | 3 | 4 | 5 | 6 | 7 | 8 |

My One-Minute Math Tests          Winthrop

Date   Color the number you did correctly in one minute.

| Date | | | | | | | | |
|------|--|--|--|--|--|--|--|--|
| Feb. 3 | 1 | 2 | 3 | 4 | 5 | 6 | 7 | 8 |

# Motor Progress Charts

Select five motor skills. Make a set of five cards for each child and write one motor skill on each card.

When the children complete a day's work on a specific motor skill, have them record their best score on the appropriate card.

Note the child's most recent progress by comparing the final score with the one immediately preceding it. The scores read from left to right and line by line.

# Reading Progress Tapes

Tape recordings offer dramatic proof of children's progress. This is especially so when a child compares the first recording of his or her reading with the last one made.

Have each child bring a blank cassette tape from home. Write the child's name, the name of the school, and the year on the cassette. Provide a cassette holder for storing the children's cassettes in the classroom.

For recording reading progress, have the children prepare and tape a short oral reading each month.

Hearing their voices on tape can initially be a strange and sometimes scary experience for children, but they rarely find it dull. Soon big smiles will emerge as each child listens to a tape that he or she can keep forever.

Help the children compare their readings and note improvements. At the end of the year, play the child's first and last tape recordings. The improvement will give him or her a sense of achievement.

**Using a tape recorder.** With a few instructions, any school-aged child can learn to use a tape recorder.

Facilitate usage for nonreaders by marking the stop and start buttons with a large red or green dot.

Explain that tapes can be reused but that when this is done, you lose what was initially recorded. Then, tell the children that because you don't want to lose any important recordings, only you and the special cross-age or parent helpers will rewind a tape. Also announce that you will tape this reminder to a visible spot on the tape recorder. The precautionary reminder to the children is *Don't rewind the tape.*

You are apt to have at least one child in each class who is particularly adept with machines. Emphasize this talent by appointing him or her to be the tape recorder expert. Suggest that, when necessary, the other children ask the "expert" how to use the tape recorder. You will spare yourself numerous questions and also encourage peer responsibility for sharing functional knowledge.

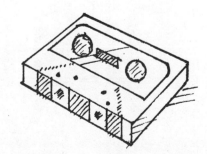

This chart helps children see their progress in mastering the letters of the alphabet.

Duplicate this page and give one chart to each child. Suggest that the children color the appropriately lettered block as soon as they are able to recognize, pronounce, and print that letter of the alphabet.

# My Alphabet Record

by _____

# Word Mastery Boxes

If you have a small class and adequate storage space, consider this activity for recording the mastery of new spelling or reading words.

Have each child bring a shoe box from home. Help the children prepare alphabetical dividers from tagboard. Provide alphabet tabs but have the children attach them to the dividers with transparent tape. (Tabs are available at stationery stores but are also easily made from tagboard or manila folders.)

Help the children alphabetize the dividers for placement in the shoe boxes.

As each spelling or reading word is mastered, ask the children to print the word on a card (sized to fit the shoe boxes) and to file the card or piece of paper in the appropriate alphabetical section.

**Using notebooks.** As an alternative to shoe boxes, have the children bring small spiral-bound notebooks to school. Divide each notebook into twenty-six parts and write an alphabet letter at the top of the first page in each part. Then, under the appropriate letter in the notebook, have the children print the words that they master.

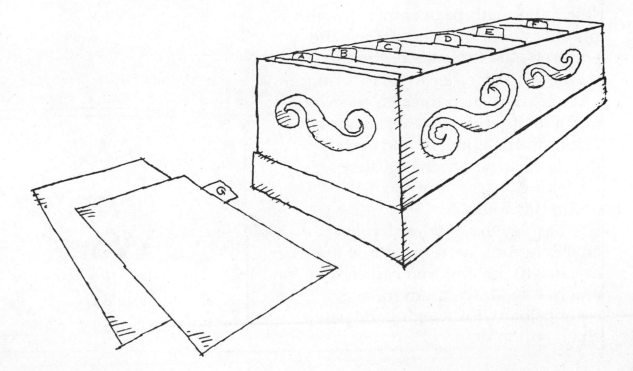

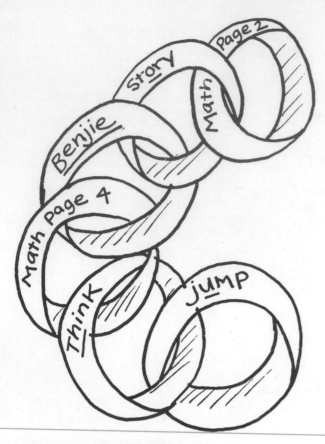

# Favorite-Work Folders

Have the children fold in half lengthwise a 14″ x 20″ piece of paper that they have decorated. Punch several evenly spaced holes on both short sides of the folded paper. Ask the children to use an overcast stitch and sew the folder sides together with cord or yarn. (Or simply staple the sides of the folders together.) Provide assistance as needed.

Invite the children to print *My Favorite-Work Folder* and their names on the folders. (Or print this for them.)

Decorate a box in which to store the *Favorite-Work Folders.*

When a child does particularly good work or seems to enjoy a project more than usual, ask if he or she wants to save the paper. Once a month, ask the children to select and put one of these papers into their *Favorite-Work Folder.*

# Paper Chains

Stock the activity center with numerous 1″ x 5″ paper strips. As the children complete academic work, have them write on a paper strip the name of the book, the word, the math page completed, the phonics sound mastered. Have the children glue the ends of their first paper strip together to form a ring. Pass the next strip through the ring and glue its ends together to begin a chain. As the children add each new link to their paper chains, they will have tangible proof of their accomplishments.

Display the children's paper chains in the classroom. Place them at a height the children can easily reach. Encourage them to take responsibility for keeping the paper chains up-to-date.

Have the children complete this evaluation questionnaire at the conclusion of each major activity. Read the queries aloud so that nonreaders can also fill out the forms.

Save the questionnaires so each child can later compare his or her behavior records and see the improvement.

In addition, use the questionnaires to help you evaluate the appropriateness of your assignments and to alert you to times when a child is distressed.

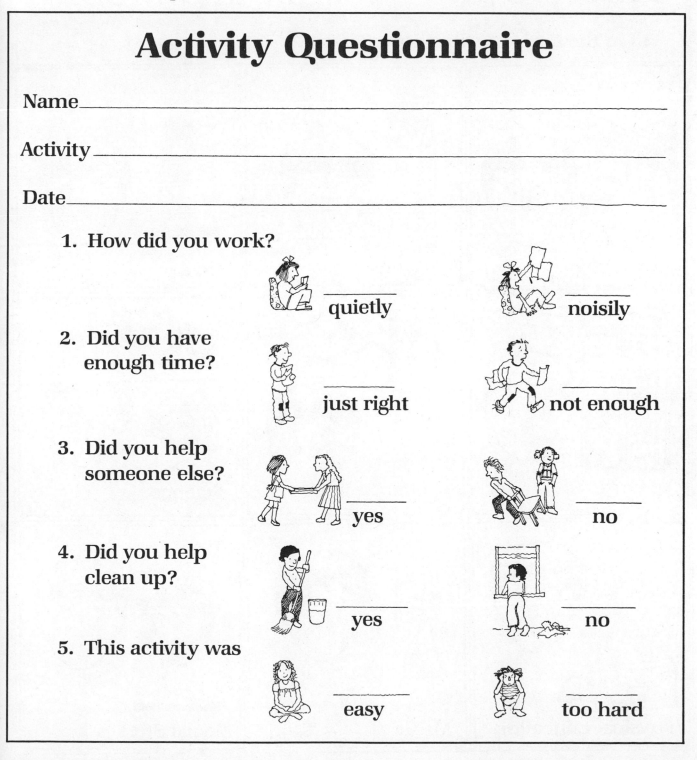

# Activity Questionnaire

Name_____

Activity_____

Date_____

1.  How did you work?

    _____ quietly                    _____ noisily

2.  Did you have
    enough time?

    _____ just right                 _____ not enough

3.  Did you help
    someone else?

    _____ yes                        _____ no

4.  Did you help
    clean up?

    _____ yes                        _____ no

5.  This activity was

    _____ easy                       _____ too hard

The next two charts help children become aware of their feelings about what they are studying. It also gives you an indication of why the children in your classroom may be doing well or poorly in their academic work.

Duplicate the chart on this page and have the children fill in the faces to show how they feel.

# How Do You Feel About School?

Fill in the faces to show how you feel.

Reading

Writing

Math

Art

Spelling

Science

Physical Education

Music

Social Studies

 *Self-Esteem: A Classroom Affair,* © 1978, Winston Press, Inc.

The way people feel shows in their faces. Adults often learn to hide feelings, but children tend not to cover them up.

Have the children look in a mirror and make their faces show feelings, such as fear, anger, sadness, happiness, pride.

Then ask the children to sketch the way they think they look in the situations indicated on this page.

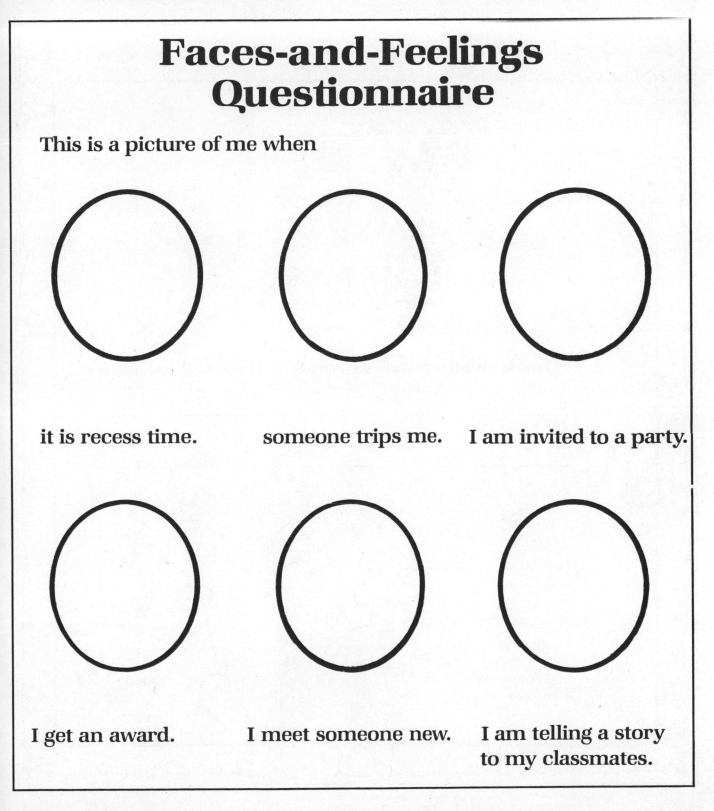

# Faces-and-Feelings Questionnaire

This is a picture of me when

it is recess time.

someone trips me.

I am invited to a party.

I get an award.

I meet someone new.

I am telling a story to my classmates.

# Give Awards

We feel that certificates and awards for behavior and for academic accomplishments are extremely important because they draw attention to a child's progress and encourage people to compliment the child.

When you talk to the children's parents, share with them how important you think it is for children to see their awards displayed at home.

# Award -O- Gram

This special award is proudly presented to

_____

for _____

signed _____

_____

date _____

**The happygram is a special award form.  Use it as often as you can.**

# happygram

I am happy to announce that

_____

has learned to

_____

And are
we
proud!

date _____

signed _____

# A Letter to Encourage and Support

Children love to receive mail, so create a happy moment for them by occasionally telling them in a letter how pleased you are with their attitudes and actions. You may want to write a letter similar to the one that illustrates this page.

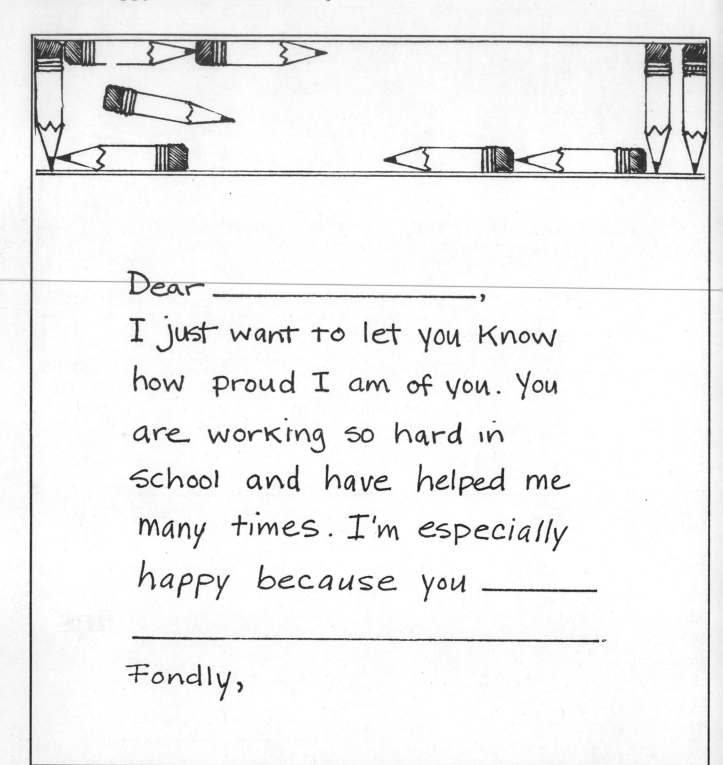

Dear _____,

I just want to let you know how proud I am of you. You are working so hard in school and have helped me many times. I'm especially happy because you _____

_____.

Fondly,

# Chapter Nine
# Bulletin Boards

In the light of the influence of the self-concept on academic achievement, it would seem like a good idea for schools to follow the precept I saw printed on an automobile drag-strip racing program: "Every effort is made to ensure that each entry has a reasonable chance of victory."

William Purkey
*Self-Concept and School Achievement*

---

# Using Bulletin Boards

Background material for these bulletin board activities can often be developed in concept circles. Some of the circles discussed in "Concept Circles," pages 51-72, correlate well with these activities. Or you may want to call the children together in a circle simply to give instructions and to begin thinking about a new bulletin board activity.

# Self-Discoveries

## I'm Glad to Be Me

Encourage pride in children's self-discoveries by having them write I'm-glad-to-be-me statements to accompany self-portraits on a bulletin board.

Cut out 8″ circles of flesh-colored construction paper. Have each child decorate a circle to look like his or her face. Suggest they attach yarn for hair, and color in the eyes, mouth, nose, and freckles. Pin these self-portraits onto a bulletin board headed by the words *I'm glad to be me!*

Then, ask the children to complete the statement *I'm glad to be me because. . . .* Print the children's statements on 2″ x 6″ strips of paper and mount each statement under the appropriate face on the bulletin board.

favorite TV show, book, pet, food, song, school subject, place, game, toy, singer, day of the week, hobby. On the chalkboard, write the children's ideas in the form of questions; for example, Who is your favorite singer?

Duplicate the chalkboard list of questions, give a copy to each child, and have him or her answer the questions.

Tabulate the answers and post an announcement of the group's favorite things on the bulletin board. Decorate the board with drawings of the children's favorite things.

# Our Favorite Things

Favorite things reflect personal choices and reveal identity. Reinforce children's self-awareness by making a bulletin board of favorite things.

First, cut out and post on the board the words *Our Favorite Things!* Make two blue-ribbon awards and post these beside the words.

Then, begin to collect information for the bulletin board by asking the children to decide what they want to learn about each other. The children may want to know such things as the group's

# The Inn of Friendliness

Use the *Inn-of-Friendliness* bulletin board to motivate friendly actions. Acknowledging children's positive actions encourages healthy pride.

Enlarge the pattern on the next page and construct an *Inn of Friendliness* to fit your bulletin board. Mount the inn on an appropriate background. Explain to the children that this inn will give them the opportunity to award each other for friendly actions.

Ask your students to observe their classmates' friendly actions and write the names of those who do friendly things on the entrance, which is located between the *Inn-of-Friendliness* doors. Each day, acknowledge that day's friendly actions by stapling or pinning a new list to the entrance.

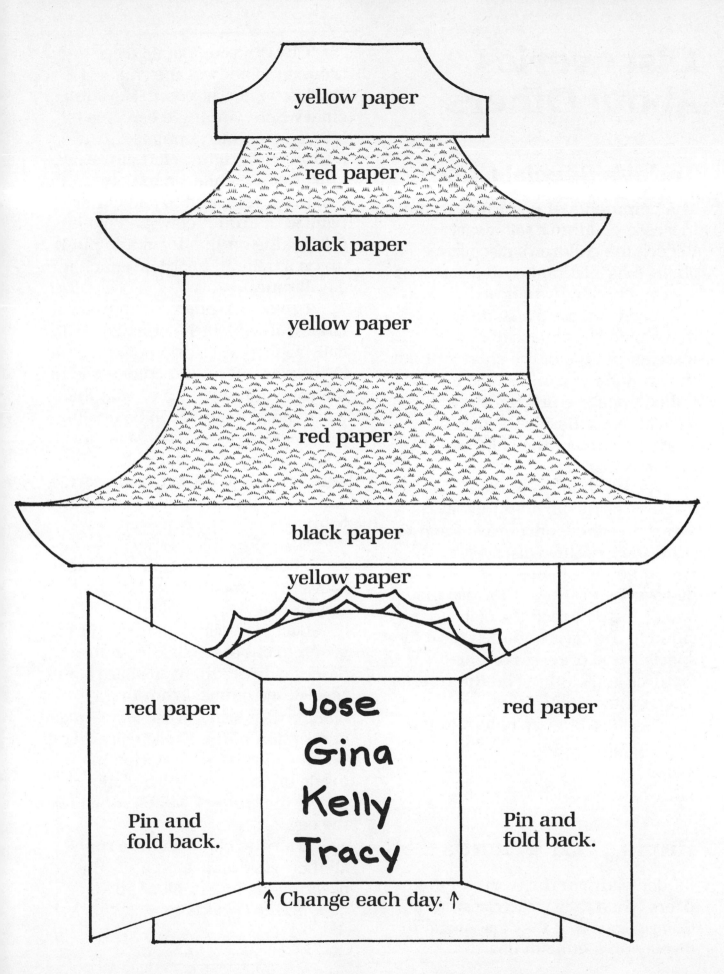

yellow paper

red paper

black paper

yellow paper

red paper

black paper

yellow paper

red paper

red paper

Jose
Gina
Kelly
Tracy

Pin and
fold back.

Pin and
fold back.

↑ Change each day. ↑

# Discoveries About Others

## Today's Special Child

The comments of peers and friends increase children's self-awareness. Record the children's discoveries about their classmates in a series of special-child bulletin boards.

Each day, have a student lie down on a large piece of paper; trace an outline of the child. Cut out the outline form and staple it to a bulletin board entitled *Today's Special Child.* Beside the cutout, post the name of the child being honored that day.

As the children make discoveries throughout the day about this child, encourage them to print their positive discoveries on the cutout. (Or print their discoveries for them.) Toward the end of the day, read the discoveries aloud to the class and then have the special child draw his or her features and clothing on the reverse side of the cutout.

Give the life-size cutout to the child to take home.

## Roping Our Friends

Students affirm the worth of their peers when they write classmate descriptions that they are proud to display on a bulletin board.

On wrapping paper, trace around the body of the smallest child in your classroom. Have the child whom you trace bend his or her right arm to simulate throwing a lariat from right to left at waist level. Ask the children to paint in the child's features and to add either painted or cutout cowhand clothing. Cut out the outline form and pin it up on a bulletin board or attach it to a wall mural.

Use clothesline cord to make a lariat with which the cowhand will daily rope a description of one child in the classroom. Attach one end of the rope to the cutout so that the cowhand will appear to be holding and throwing the lariat. Make a noose at the other end of the rope and attach it to the bulletin board or wall mural in the shape of a picture frame.

Have the children decorate the remainder of the bulletin board or mural with appropriate hills and trees.

Each day, ask the children as a group to choose a classmate to describe. Invite them to share aloud their descriptions. From the children's sharing, write a one-page description of the chosen classmate. When you post the description inside the lariat on the bulletin board, the student will be roped for the day.

After the children have roped all their classmates, compile the descriptions in a book entitled *Roping Our Friends.*

# V.I.P. Board

The *V.I.P.* bulletin board affirms each child's importance and acknowledges his or her right to self-pride by centering classmates' attention on him or her for several days or for a full week.

Begin this continuing bulletin board after sufficient time has passed in the school year for the children to have won some awards.

When you introduce this bulletin board activity, explain to the children that V.I.P. means *Very Important Person.* Discuss some of the things that make a person important. Then select the first class *V.I.P.*

Ask the *V.I.P.'s* parents to provide photographs of him or her in various stages of his or her development. Display the photos, the awards the child has received, and samples of his or her hobbies or special interests.

Continue the *V.I.P.* bulletin board until you've honored each child in your room.

# Who's Who-o-o?

Use this bulletin board activity to give the children practice in recalling personal facts and features that they can use in writing riddles about themselves.

First, attach a real tree branch to the bulletin board. Draw and cut out a large owl from heavy tagboard. Set the owl on the branch.

Have each child write or dictate a riddle about him or herself. Fold the riddles and put them into a small sack. Hang the sack of riddles from the branch.

Cut out colored letters and title the bulletin board *Who's Who-o-o?* Make a construction paper talk bubble (as seen in cartoon strips) for each child in the classroom. Pin the talk bubbles onto the bulletin board.

Each day, draw a different riddle out of the sack, ask a volunteer to read the riddle, and have the children guess who the mystery child is. When they've guessed, pin the riddle onto a bubble on the bulletin board.

# Hands Around the World

Emphasize self-awareness by having the children first fingerpaint a globe on a sheet of wrapping paper which will become the bulletin board background. Add the theme sentence *We have the whole world in our hands!*

Next, have each child trace around his or her hand and cut out the tracing. Have each child print his or her name on the palm of the cutout hand. On each finger, ask him or her to write a different word that describes him or herself, such as *smiles, shares, hugs, friendly, quiet, grumpy.*

Pin or paste the friendly hands around the globe.

# Friendly Flower Blossoms

Drawing attention to children's friendly behavior will help them feel good about themselves and confirm their sense of self-worth.

Have the children paint the trunk and branches of a tree on a large sheet of paper that will become the bulletin board background. Beside the tree trunk, or underneath it, add the words *The Friendship Tree.* On colored paper, duplicate flower blossoms and ask the children to cut them out.

On the flower blossoms, write friendly actions you observe, such as John smiled at Kari or Amy shared her crayons with Nathan. Pin or paste the flower blossoms to the tree branches. Emphasize the person who did the friendly action by underlining his or her name or by writing it larger than the rest of the words in the statement.

# Our Community

When children make replicas of their houses and describe them, they develop awareness of family uniqueness. The children expand self-awareness into social awareness by placing the houses on a bulletin board that suggests coexistence in a community.

First, have the children make the bulletin board background by painting trees, sun, clouds, and flowers on an appropriately sized paper. Staple the background to the bulletin board. At the top of the bulletin board, add the words *Our Community.*

Then have each child make a book cover in the shape of his or her house. To represent the bottom of the house, have each child cut out a 9″ square of construction paper that is the same color as his or her house. For the roof, have the children attach a 6″ x 9″ triangle cut from brown construction paper. Suggest that the children add doors and windows cut from paper scraps and ask each child to write his or her name above the house door.

Make book pages the same shape as the cover. Provide sufficient pages so the children have a separate page on which to describe each room of their individual houses. Staple together the pages and cover of each child's book. Pin the books to the bulletin board.

# Class Discoveries

## Classroom-Friends Quilt

Increase children's self-awareness by having them make fabric self-portraits, which can be sewn together to make a classroom-friends quilt.

## Materials Needed

- 8″ flesh-colored felt circles
- buttons
- lace
- yarn
- rickrack
- sewing-trim braid
- large-eye needles
- various-colored embroidery thread
- various-colored felt scraps
- pipe cleaners
- pinking shears
- scissors
- 12″ squares of burlap
- #10 sewing thread

Have each child decorate an eight-inch, flesh-colored felt circle to look like his or her face. Suggest that the children use red felt circles for cheeks, yarn for hair, buttons or felt circles for eyes, and felt scraps for mouths. Or suggest running stitches for mouths and eyebrows, and french knots for freckles. (Have the children first practice sewing running stitches and making french knots on pieces of scrap fabric.) Use pipe cleaners for glasses. Add lace, rickrack, or braid for collars, and yarn bows for hair ribbons.

On one or two burlap squares, embroider or glue on felt letters for the words *Classroom Friends.*

Have each child sew or glue his or her finished felt circle-face to a burlap square. With pinking shears, pink around the edges of each burlap square to prevent raveling. Or zigzag a row of stay stitching around the edges.

Arrange the squares in a shape to fit your bulletin board and sew the squares of faces together to make a bulletin-board quilt. (You may want to ask a parent helper to do this sewing.)

Pin the quilt of classmates' faces to the bulletin board.

## The Class Soldier Salutes You

Completing goals increases a child's sense of accomplishment and self-worth. Draw attention to this achievement with a bulletin board.

On construction paper, draw a large wooden soldier in saluting position. Pin the soldier to one end of a bulletin board. Add the words *The Class Soldier Salutes You!* at the top of the board.

Then, prepare colorful, two-inch construction paper circles. As each child completes a task, write the task and his or her name on a circle. Pin the circle to the board and run a ribbon or cord from the saluting soldier to the children's circles.

# How We Feel About Important Things

Use a bulletin board activity to help children identify how they feel about different topics, such as school, recess, reading, friends, home, themselves. Identifying how they feel is an important step for the children in their journey toward self-discovery.

At the top of the bulletin board post the words *How I Feel About Important Things.* Underneath these words, place daily a card that indicates the topic about which you will ask the children to share their feelings on that day. In the center of the board, pin up a large arrow. Around it, pin up five faces that are individually labeled *happy, sad, scared, angry,* or *proud.*

Each day, ask the children, "How do you feel about . . ." and complete the question with a topic.

Duplicate the feeling faces on a ballot like the one here and have each child color the face that shows how he or she feels about the topic under discussion.

Help the children tabulate the classroom results. Then, point the arrow toward the bulletin board face that received the most votes.

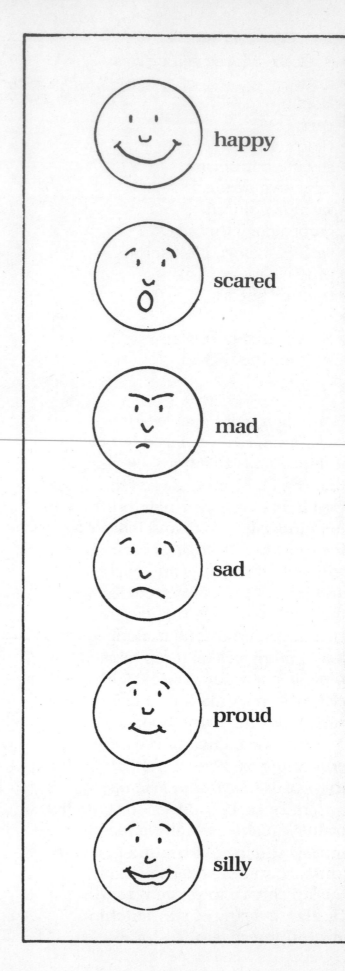

happy

scared

mad

sad

proud

silly

All the flowers of all the tomorrows
are in the seeds of today.

Ancient Chinese proverb

# Parent Enthusiasm

Involving parents in classroom activities helps them become enthusiastic about what's happening in their child's school. This parent enthusiasm is contagious—it can be "caught" by the children, the other parents, and you! All of you will then be happier as you create a more supportive atmosphere for learning. To get parents involved, consider using the following ideas:

- Keep communication flowing! Whenever you begin a new project, send home a note explaining its purpose and how parents can provide support and reinforcement.

- Provide parents with a list of games and activities that they can do at home and that will encourage their child's affective and academic growth.

- Invite parents to become parent helpers and to help you prepare for daily classroom activities at after-school work sessions.

- Have parent helpers arrange a parent get-together at one of their homes. Include yourself. The informal atmosphere will encourage getting better acquainted.

- A few times each year, have after-school parent discussions. Explain your current goals, new materials, and ways parents can help at home.

- Plan to have one home conference with each of your students' families during the year. The proud smiles on your students' faces when they show you their homes will be well worth your time.

# Letter and Supply Checklist for Parents

Parents are often willing to provide additional supplies for your activity centers. Duplicate this letter and the parent checklist, send them home with each child, and file the replies for filling future needs.

Dear Parent,

This year we'll begin studying why all of us are very special people. We'll learn some things about who we are, why we are special, what our feelings are, and how we are like other people.

On the enclosed parent checklist, we've enumerated some of the things we'll need in our activity center. Can you help us? Check materials you'd like to donate, and return the letter with your child tomorrow. When we have use for an item you've checked, we'll contact you. Thanks.

Sincerely,

*Self-Esteem: A Classroom Affair,* © 1978, Winston Press, Inc.    Permission is given to reproduce this page for student use.

# Supply Checklist for Parents

I can provide the following materials upon request:

_____ sequins
_____ rickrack
_____ lace
_____ buttons
_____ yarn
_____ wallpaper remnants or books
_____ felt scraps
_____ burlap
_____ fabric
_____ catalogs
_____ glitter
_____ felt-tip markers
_____ felt pens
_____ wrapped presents
_____ sunglasses
_____ hand mirror
_____ a crown
_____ brass rings
_____ magazines
_____ blindfolds
_____ a timer
_____ hats
_____ telephones (play or real)
_____ calendar pictures
_____ a microphone (for pretending with)
_____ cotton batting or cotton balls
_____ colorful scarves
_____ clothes hangers
_____ large-eye needles
_____ #10 sewing thread
_____ telephone book

_____
(Parent's signature)

_____
(Date)

# Parent Helpers

Children respond positively to the interest, love, and concern of parent helpers. With minimal training, parent helpers can take over some activity supervision and free you to spend more time helping children with special needs, conducting private student conferences, and initiating new projects.

Before inviting parents to become classroom helpers, make a list of the activities other adults can do in your room. Possible activities might be special art projects, cooking, tutoring, reading with a child, motor skill practice. When you are sure about the things you want help with, write and duplicate a letter requesting helpers for these activities and send the letter home with each child. Facilitate cooperation by clearly stating the time and date of the work sessions in your request letter. (See parent-helper request letters on pages 125 and 127.)

If you prefer not to have the parents of your students work in your classroom, consider parent helpers from another class or volunteer aides from the PTA or a nearby college (particularly the psychology, child development, and sociology classes).

Arrange an after-school meeting to welcome prospective parent helpers and to introduce yourself. Acquaint them with the classroom and its facilities, including the location of supplies.

Explain your goals and tell the parent helpers how their assistance will meet needs you cannot cope with alone.

Then, ask the parents to write down their names and phone numbers, the activities in which they have particular interest, their special qualifications, and times convenient for them to assist in the classroom. Point out that it is vital to your program that parent helpers be dependable.

To prepare your room for the daily presence of parent helpers, designate a place where the helpers can find the project materials they will need for assisting you that day. (Be sure to put the materials out ahead of time!) Also place two notebooks in the helper area. In one, write special instructions for the parent helpers to use in working with the children. Encourage the parent helpers to use the second notebook for writing down questions they have, observations they've made about a child, and statements regarding their availability for future sessions.

Suggest to your students that they show their appreciation to these special helpers by giving them handmade cards or original drawings in addition to saying "thank you."

# Parent-Helper Letter

This reproducible letter is an invitation to parents to participate in their child's learning experience by being a parent helper and assisting with classroom activities.

Dear Parents,

Many things are happening in our classroom. We're working hard to learn several new concepts. It's a joy for me to work with such a delightful group. If their enthusiasm remains as high as it is now, we'll literally sail through the year.

You can be an important part of this learning process, too! We'd love to have you participate. If you can help us in any of the ways listed below, please check the item(s) and return the checklist with your child tomorrow. Feel free to add other ways you'd like to help the children.

_____ assist in the classroom an hour each week

_____ make activity items at home

_____ run off dittos at school

_____ correct student work at home

_____ help in the stitchery center

_____ help in the cooking center

_____ help in the carpentry center

_____ provide transportation on field trips

_____ make treats for class parties

_____ relay parent messages by phone

_____ share special knowledge with the children. For example: present a science experiment, read poetry, show slides of a foreign country or another state, exhibit and talk about a hobby.

Sincerely,

# Reading Party

One of the greatest joys we experience in teaching is to hear the exuberant words *I can read!* Celebrate this event with a reading party to which the children invite parents or other special persons. Have each child choose a favorite story or book to read to his or her guest. Discuss the party with the children and help them practice what they will read.

**Sending invitations.** Duplicate the invitation below, have the children fill in the missing information, and mail the invitations to parents or other special persons. Or ask the children to take the invitations home and give them to their parents or to another special person.

**Decorating the room.** Divide the class into three groups. Provide sufficient cake for the party, a cake decorating set, and frosting ingredients. The morning of the party have one group decorate the cake. Divide the decorating chores among the children in the group.

Have the second group decorate white napkins by drawing pictures of their favorite storybook characters on the napkins with crayons or colored pens.

For a lovely tablecloth, have the third group decorate a large piece of butcher paper with the same storybook characters being used to decorate the napkins.

**Making bookmarkers.** After the children have read for their guests, suggest that each child ask his or her guest of honor to join him or her in making a felt bookmarker. (Be sure the activity center is well supplied with felt, rickrack, sequins, glitter, glue, and scissors.) Invite each child to take the bookmarker home and use it in a favorite book that he or she will read with a parent or a special friend.

Come to our <u>Reading Party</u> and hear me read! Please come!

Place _____

Date _____

Time _____

Signed _____

# Parent Letter About Children's Progress

This letter will keep parents in touch with their child's academic progress and solicit parental help and support. Add your telephone number after your signature.

Dear Parent,

You can be very proud of your child's hard work. _____ is now studying _____

_____

_____

You can support and reinforce what _____ is learning by _____

_____

_____

_____

If you have any questions or comments, please feel free to write or call me. Thank you for your cooperation and for encouraging _____ to do so well.

Sincerely,

# Spring Open House

Duplicate the open-house program below. It depicts nine of this book's major projects, which your students will have completed during the year. Ask parents to tour the classroom with their child and listen attentively to his or her comments about each project.

Dear Parent,

This is your official program for tonight. The children are excited about your visit and want to make sure you see everything they've done during the year. I know you'll be just as proud as the children are. As your child shows you each project, place a check mark in the square by the appropriate activity picture. Have fun!

Read a story aloud.

Look through your *Favorite-Work Folder*.

Read your *Who's Who-o-o?* riddle.

Show your *Favorite-Activities* mobile.

Show your *What-I-Can-Do* book.

Recipe for Nancy
2 tbsp. niceness
1 tsp. naughtiness
dash of smiles
a few hugs
Mix the niceness and naughtiness. Add a dash of smiles and a few hugs. Bake well in the love and care of friends and of family.

Read the *People Recipe* about yourself.

Show your *All-About-Me-and-My-Feelings* book.

Have your puppet talk to your visitor.

Tell about your favorite *Talking Box* activity.

 *Self-Esteem: A Classroom Affair,* © 1978, Winston Press, Inc.

Recognize the efforts parents expend doing things for you and your students by giving them this award at a special classroom event.

# Super-Parent Award

### This award is fondly given to

_____

for _____

_____

signed _____

date _____

# Appendix

## A Piece of Clay

I took a piece of living clay
    And gently formed it day by day
And moulded with my press and art
    A young child's soft and yielding heart.

I came again when years were gone,
    It was a man I looked upon.
He still that early impress wore,
    And I could change it never more.

I took a piece of plastic clay
    And idly fashioned it one day.
And as my fingers pressed it still,
    It moved and yielded to my will.

I came again when days were past,
    The feel of clay was hard at last.
The form I gave, it still bore;
    But I could change that form no more.

Anonymous

132

# Bibliotherapy for Children

Reading books to young students is one of the nicest gifts a teacher can give, and watching the children's expressions change as they visualize characters' thoughts and actions is a delightful experience for the teacher.

Children need a great variety of experiences for basic psychological growth. By reading books, children can vicariously increase their range of experiences. It is in this context that we use the term *bibliotherapy*. Since children identify strongly with storybook characters, teachers can positively influence children's self-image development by careful book selection. For example, Martha Alexander's book *Sabrina* is a story of a child's embarrassment over her name and how she learns to be proud of the special name. Reading this book could help a child who is experiencing similar feelings of embarrassment and could help other children learn to understand and to respect the feelings of friends who don't like their names.

Bibliotherapy can also help children learn to feel better about physical characteristics, about family or peer relationships, and about the way they feel, think, and act.

Books are particularly helpful in assisting children to accept and to cope with limitations. As children identify with the characters, they begin to realize that they too are worthwhile persons and then continue to model their attitudes and behavior after those of the book characters.

Leland Jacobs said, "Children need literature to try on life for size."[1] We agree.

Alexander, Martha G. *And My Mean Old Mother Will Be Sorry, Blackboard Bear.* New York: Dial, 1972. (Running away)

Alexander, Martha G. *Sabrina.* New York: Dial, 1971. (Embarrassment about name)

Anglund, Joan W. *A Friend Is Someone Who Likes You.* New York: Harcourt Brace Jovanovich, 1958. (Friends)

Anglund, Joan W. *Love Is a Special Way of Feeling.* New York: Harcourt Brace Jovanovich, 1960. (Love)

Anglund, Joan W. *What Color Is Love.* New York: Harcourt Brace Jovanovich, 1966. (Love)

Barkin, Carol, and James, Elizabeth. *Sometimes I Hate School.* Milwaukee, Wis.: Raintree, 1975. (Feelings about school)

1. Leland B. Jacobs, "Teaching Children More About Words and Their Ways," *Elementary English* (October 1968):35.

Beim, Jerrold. *Smallest Boy in the Class.* New York: Wm. Morrow, 1949. (Feelings about being small)

Beim, Lorraine, and Beim, Jerrold. *Two Is a Team.* New York: Harcourt Brace Jovanovich, 1945, 1974. (Teamwork between black and white boys)

Bel Geddes, Barbara. *I Like to Be Me.* New York: Simon & Schuster, Young Readers Press, 1963. (Positive self-image)

Bemelmans, Ludwig. *Madeline.* New York: Viking, 1969; Penguin, 1977. (Sickness)

Berger, Terry. *How Does It Feel When Your Parents Get Divorced?* New York: Julian Messner, 1977. (Parental divorce)

Berger, Terry. *I Have Feelings.* New York: Human Sciences Press, 1971. (Emotions)

Blume, Judy. *Freckle Juice.* New York: Four Winds Press, Scholastic Book Services, 1971. (Feelings about having freckles)

Bonsall, Crosby N. *It's Mine!* New York: Harper & Row, 1964. (Sharing)

Breinburg, Petronella. *Shawn Goes to School.* New York: Thomas Y. Crowell, 1974. (Feelings about growing)

Buringham, John. *Mr. Grumpy's Outing.* New York: Holt, Rinehart & Winston, 1971. (Emotions)

Caines, Jeanette. *Abby.* New York: Harper & Row, 1973. (Adoption)

Charlip, Remy, and Supree, Burton. *Mother Mother I Feel Sick, Send for the Doctor Quick Quick Quick.* New York: Parents' Magazine Press, 1966. (Illness)

Clifton, Lucille. *The Boy Who Didn't Believe in Spring.* New York: E. P. Dutton, 1973. (Black child in a ghetto)

Cohen, Miriam. *Best Friends.* New York: Macmillan, Collier Books, 1973. (Friends)

Cohen, Miriam. *The New Teacher.* New York: Macmillan, Collier Books, 1974. (Insecurity over a mid-year change of teachers)

Cohen, Miriam. *Will I Have a Friend?* New York: Macmillan, Collier Books, 1971. (Friends)

Daringer, Helen. *Adopted Jane.* New York: Harcourt Brace Jovanovich, 1973. (Adoption)

De Angeli, Marguerite. *Bright April.* New York: Doubleday, 1946. (Prejudice against black girl)

De Paola, Tomie. *Nana Upstairs and Nana Downstairs.* New York: Putnam, 1973. (Death of grandmother)

De Regniers, Beatrice S. *May I Bring a Friend?* New York: Atheneum, 1974. (Friends)

Estes, Eleanor. *The Hundred Dresses.* New York: Harcourt Brace Jovanovich, 1974. (Rejection and poverty)

Ets, Marie H. *Gilberto and the Wind.* New York: Viking, 1963. (Mexican child)

Fassler, Joan. *One Little Girl.* New York: Human Sciences Press, 1969. (Mental retardation)

Gibbons, Julie. *There Is Only One Me.* Los Angeles: Science of Mind, 1974. (Specialness)

Hanson, Joan. *Alfred Snood.* New York: Putnam, 1972. (Being naughty)

Haywood, Carolyn. *Eddie and the Fire Engine.* New York: Wm. Morrow, 1949. (Missing teeth)

Heide, Florence. *Some Things Are Scary.* New York: Scholastic Book Services, 1971. (Fear)

Hitte, Kathryn. *Boy Was I Mad.* New York: Parents' Magazine Press, 1969. (Anger)

Justus, May. *New Boy in School.* New York: Hastings House, 1963. (Insecurity)

Keats, Ezra J., and Cherr, Pat. *My Dog Is Lost.* New York: Thomas Y. Crowell, 1960. (Puerto Rican child)

Kingman, Lee. *Peter's Long Walk.* New York: Doubleday, 1953. (Emotions)

Kottler, Dorothy, and Willis, Eleanor. *I Really Like Myself.* Nashville, Tenn.: Aurora, 1974. (Positive self-image)

Krasilovsky, Phyllis. *Shy Little Girl.* New York: Houghton Mifflin, 1970. (Shyness)

Krasilovsky, Phyllis. *Very Tall Little Girl.* New York: Doubleday, 1969. (Insecurity about height)

Lasker, Joe. *He's My Brother.* Chicago: Whitman, 1974. (Learning disabilities)

Levine, Edna S. *Lisa and Her Soundless World.* New York: Human Sciences Press, 1974. (Deafness)

Lexau, Joan M. *Benjie.* New York: Dial, 1964. (Shyness)

Lexau, Joan M. *Emily & the Kluncky Baby & the Next-Door Dog.* New York: Dial, 1972. (Divorce)

Lionni, Leo. *Frederick.* New York: Random House, Pantheon Books, 1967. (Values and valuing)

McGinley, Phyllis. *The Plain Princess.* Philadelphia, Pa.: Lippincott, 1945. (Feelings about being plain)

Mannheim, Grete. *Two Friends.* New York: Alfred A. Knopf, 1968. (First day of school)

Mayer, Mercer. *There's a Nightmare in My Closet.* New York: Dial, 1976. (Facing fear)

Pinkwater, Manus. *Fat Elliot and the Gorilla.* New York: Scholastic Book Services, 1974. (Feelings about being plump)

Preston, Edna. *Temper Tantrum Book.* New York: Viking, 1969. (Anger)

Randall, Blossom E. *Fun for Chris.* Chicago: Whitman, 1956. (Color difference)

Raskin, Ellen. *Spectacles.* New York: Atheneum, 1974 (Insecurity about wearing glasses)

Schick, Eleanor. *Peggy's New Brother.* New York: Macmillan, 1970. (Babies)

Shay, Arthur. *What Happens When You Go to the Hospital.* Chicago: Contemporary Books. 1969. (Illness)

Shay, Arthur. *What Happens When You Mail a Letter.* Chicago: Contemporary Books, 1967. (Postal service)

Shay, Arthur. *What Happens When You Make a Telephone Call.* Chicago: Contemporary Books, 1968. (Telephoning)

Simon, Norma. *How Do I Feel.* Chicago: Whitman, 1970. (Twins with different feelings)

Simon, Norma. *I Was So Mad!* Chicago: Whitman, 1974. (Understanding and expressing anger)

Viorst, Judith. *Alexander and the Terrible Horrible No Good Very Bad Day.* New York: Atheneum, 1976. (Coping with good and bad days)

Viorst, Judith. *Tenth Good Thing About Barney.* New York: Atheneum, 1971. (Death of a pet)

Waber, Bernard. *Ira Sleeps Over.* New York: Houghton Mifflin, 1972. (Insecurity)

Watson, Jean W. *Look at Me Now.* Racine, Wis.: Western, Golden Press, 1971. (Understanding growing up)

Waston, Jean. *Sometimes I Get Angry.* Racine, Wis.: Western, Golden Press, 1971. (Anger)

Watson, Jean W. *Sometimes I'm Afraid.* Racine, Wis.: Western, Golden Press, 1971. (Fear)

Wells, Rosemary. *Noisy Nora.* New York: Scholastic Book Services, 1976. (Feelings about rejection)

Wolf, Bernard. *Don't Feel Sorry for Paul.* Philadelphia, Pa.: Lippincott, 1974. (Handicapped limbs)

Wolff, Angelika. *Mom! I Broke My Arm!* New York: Lion Press, 1969. (Accidents)

Wolff, Angelika. *Mom! I Need Glasses!* New York: Lion Press, 1970. (Wearing glasses)

Zolotow, Charlotte. *The Hating Book.* New York: Harper & Row, 1969. (Feelings of rejection and anger)

Zolotow, Charlotte. *The Quarreling Book.* New York: Harper & Row, 1963. (Fighting)

Zolotow, Charlotte. *The Storm Book.* New York: Harper & Row, 1952. (Fear of storms)

Zolotow, Charlotte. *William's Doll.* Harper & Row, 1972. (Feelings about boys who cry)

# Bibliography— Primarily for Adults

Axline, Virginia M. *Dibs: In Search of Self.* New York Random House, Ballantine Books, 1976.

Branden, Nathaniel. *Psychology of Self-Esteem.* New York: Bantam, 1971.

Briggs, Dorothy Corkille. *Your Child's Self-Esteem.* New York: Doubleday, 1970.

Burgess, Patricia. *Erica's School on the Hill: A Child's Journey in Moral Growth.* Minneapolis- Minn.: Winston Press, 1978.

Canfield, Jack, and Wells, Harold C. *101 Ways to Enhance Self-Concept in the Classroom: A Handbook for Teachers and Parents.* Englewood Cliffs, N.J.: Prentice-Hall, 1976.

Carson, Rachel. *The Sense of Wonder.* New York: Harper & Row, 1956, 1965.

Coopersmith, Stanley. *Antecedents of Self-Esteem.* San Francisco: W. H. Freeman, 1967.

Davidson, H. H., and Lang, G. "Children's Perceptions of Their Teacher's Feelings Toward Them Related to Self-Perception, School Achievement, and Behavior." *Journal of Experimental Education* 29 (1960):107-118.

Elkind, David. *Children and Adolescents: Interpretive Essays on Jean Piaget.* 2nd ed. New York: Oxford University Press, 1974.

Fink, M. B. "Self-Concept as It Relates to Academic Underachievement." *California Journal of Educational Research* 13 (1962):57-61.

Glasser, William. *Schools Without Failure.* New York: Harper & Row, 1969, 1975.

Hamachek, Donald E. *Encounter with the Self.* New York: Holt, Rinehart & Winston, 1971.

Harmin, Merrill; Kirschenbaum, Howard; and Simon, Sidney B. *Clarifying Values Through Subject Matter: Applications for the Classroom.* Minneapolis, Minn.: Winston Press, 1973.

Hartley, Ruth E. *Understanding Children's Play.* New York: Columbia University Press, 1952.

Hawley, Robert C., and Hawley, Isabel L. *Human Values in the Classroom: Teaching for Personal and Social Growth.* New York: Hart, 1975.

Herbruck, Christine C. *Breaking the Cycle of Child Abuse.* Minneapolis, Minn.: Winston Press, 1979.

Holt, John. *How Children Learn.* New York: Dell, Delta Books, 1972.

Jacobs, Leland B., ed. *Using Literature with Young Children.* New York: Teachers College Press, 1965.

James, Muriel, and Jongeward, Dorothy. *Born to Win: Transactional Analysis with Gestalt Experiments.* Reading, Mass.: Addison-Wesley, 1971.

Jersild, Arthur T. *In Search of Self: An Exploration of the Role of the School in Promoting Self-Understanding.* New York: Teachers College Press, 1952.

Lederman, Janet. *Anger and the Rocking Chair: Gestalt Awareness with Children.* New York: Penguin, 1973.

Long, Nicholas J.; Newman, Ruth; and Morse, William C. *Conflict in the Classroom: The Education of Children with Problems.* Belmont, Calif.: Wadsworth, 1976.

MacDonald, W. Scott, and Oden, Chester W., Jr. *Moose: A Very Special Person.* Minneapolis, Minn.: Winston Press, 1978.

Moustakas, Clark. *The Authentic Teacher: Sensitivity and Awareness in the Classroom.* Cambridge, Mass.: Howard A. Doyle, 1966.

Paulson, Wayne. *The Values Corner.* Minneapolis, Minn.: Winston Press, 1976.

Piaget, Jean. *Moral Judgment of the Child.* New York: Free Press, 1932.

Piaget, Jean. *The Origins of Intelligence in Children.* New York: W. W. Norton, 1952.

*Polliwog: A Personal Development Program with Values and Reading Readiness Skills for Young Children.* Minneapolis, Minn.: Winston Press, 1976.

Purkey, William W., Sr. *Self-Concept and School Achievement.* Englewood Cliffs, N.J.: Prentice-Hall, 1970.

Rogers, Carl. *The Clinical Treatment of the Problem Child.* Boston, Mass.: Houghton Mifflin, 1939.

Samuels, Shirley C. *Enhancing Self-Concept in Early Childhood.* New York: Human Sciences Press, 1977.

Scharf, Peter, ed. *Readings in Moral Education.* Minneapolis, Minn.: Winston Press, 1977.

Scharf, Peter; McCoy, William; and Ross, Diane. *Growing Up Moral: Dilemmas for Intermediate Grades.* Minneapolis, Minn.: Winston Press, 1979.

Simon, Sidney B. *I Am Lovable and Capable.* Niles, Ill.: Argus, 1974.

Simon, Sidney B., and Kirschenbaum, Howard. *Readings in Values Clarification.* Minneapolis, Minn.: Winston Press, 1973.

Simon, Sidney B., and O'Rourke, Robert. *Developing Values with Exceptional Children.* Englewood Cliffs, N.J.: Prentice-Hall, 1977.

Simon, Sidney B.; Howe, Leland; and Kirschenbaum, Howard. *Values Clarification: A Handbook of Practical Strategies for Teachers and Students.* New York: Hart, 1972.

Sogn, Donnelen Locke. *Remember the Laughter: Children, Death, and Loss.* Minneapolis, Minn.: Winston Press, forthcoming.

Stevens, John O. *Awareness: Exploring, Experimenting, Experiencing.* New York: Bantam, 1973.

Ungaro, Daniel. *How to Create a Better Understanding of Our Schools.* Minneapolis, Minn.: T. S. Denison, 1959.

Walsh, A. M. *Self-Concepts of Bright Boys with Learning Difficulties.* New York: Teachers College Press, 1956.

Wattenberg, W., and Clifford, Clare. "Relationship of Self-Concepts to Beginning Achievement in Reading." *Child Development* 35 (1964):461-467.

Wylie, Ruth. *The Self-Concept: A Critical Survey of Pertinent Research Literature.* Lincoln, Nebr.: University of Nebraska Press, 1961.

# About the Authors

Michele Borba has her B.A. in history and her M.A. in education for the learning handicapped from Santa Clara University. Michele is a special-education teacher in Saratoga, California and a prescriptive remediation specialist for Counseling and Learning Consultants in Campbell, California. Among her several publications are the titles *About a Very Special Person . . . Me!* and *First Words for Reading.*

Craig Borba's B.S. and his M.A. in counseling psychology are from Santa Clara University. A former high school special-education teacher, Craig is now a school psychologist with the Gilroy school system and an adolescent counselor for Counseling and Learning Consultants. Included among his publications are *Preparation for Learning* and *Using the Alphabet.*

The Borbas have jointly developed and published elementary school curriculum materials in reading, writing, and arithmetic—for parents and teachers. Their newest publication is entitled *The Good Apple Guide to Learning Centers.*